UP IN SMOKE

FROM THE AUTHOR OF
CAST IRON GOURMET

UP IN SMOKE

A COMPLETE
**GUIDE TO
COOKING**
with smoke

MATT PELTON

Hobble Creek Press • An Imprint of Cedar Fort, Inc. • Springville, Utah

ISBN 13: 978-1-4621-1265-4

Published by Hobble Creek Press, an imprint of Cedar Fort, Inc.
2373 W. 700 S., Springville, UT 84663
Distributed by Cedar Fort, Inc., www.cedarfort.com

Library of Congress Cataloging-in-Publication Data on file

Cover and page design by Erica Dixon
Cover design © 2014 by Lyle Mortimer
Edited by Casey J. Winters

Printed in the United States of America

10 9 8 7 6 5 4 3 2 1

To T.

A great friend and mentor.

Thanks for all the times hanging out around the pit,
helping me learn the secrets of the Que!

CONTENTS

PREFACE   VIII

INTRODUCTION   01

CHAPTER 1

Barbecue Beginnings

CHAPTER 2

Smoking, Barbecuing, and Grilling

CHAPTER 3

Wood and Unleashing the Flavor

CHAPTER 4

Types of Barbecue Pits

CHAPTER 5

Fire Control

CHAPTER 6

Smoking Recipes and Techniques

CHAPTER 7

Barbecue Recipes and Techniques

CHAPTER 8

Barbecue Rubs, Sauces, and Marinades

CHAPTER 9

Barbecue Side Dishes and Desserts

CHAPTER 10

Competition Barbecue and Organizations

101   INDEX

104   MEASUREMENT CONVERSION CHARTS

106   ALSO BY MATT PELTON

109   ABOUT THE AUTHOR

PREFACE

When I was young, my dad bought an old refrigerator and built a smoker from it. He drilled holes in the top and put a plug-in frypan in the bottom. He would soak trout we caught in brine for a couple of days, fill the old racks in the refrigerator with the fish, and put applewood in the electric frypan. After several hours, we had smoked trout. As kids, we looked forward to this every summer—it was better than candy. The smoker was crude, but it worked. It was great for smoking fish, cheese, and jerky; however, you certainly couldn't barbecue with it.

For the majority of my growing-up years, this was what I associated as smoking. As I have become older, a whole other world of cooking with smoke has opened up to me. While doing demos on cooking wild game, a friend gave me a small but heavy offset smoker. I did not know at the time how much this would change my life. I bought charcoal and wood chips and started putting out some great barbecue—or so I thought. A couple of years later while I was doing some cooking demos at the International Sportsmen's Expo, Ole Hickory Pits approached me to try out their new (at the time) UltraQue model. For me this was a game changer. This smoker was an amazing unit capable of cooking over one hundred pounds of barbecue at once. I started cooking in it frequently. My neighbors

loved it as well because I cooked too much food for only my family to eat.

After a couple years, I thought I was pretty good at cooking up the Que. A friend of mine had started cooking competitive barbecue and invited me to come out and cook pro-division barbecue. The UltraQue would not be allowed because it used propane and an electric thermostat to maintain temperature. We decided on a Weber Smokey Mountain Cooker. My first competition out, I received a "walk" on my brisket (a "walk" is an award). Because of that I was absolutely hooked on barbecue. Later I learned how to make a drum smoker out of a fifty-five-gallon drum. The drum

worked nicely and was a set-it-and-forget-it-type of smoker. The flavors I was getting were unlike any I had ever tried. I should have been satisfied with my drums, but I wanted something bigger for the big parties that I catered. I built my stick burner, which we named "Two Tons of Fun."

My barbecue has stepped up to a whole new level. Barbecue sauce now runs through my blood. If I am not cooking barbecue, I am dreaming about cooking barbecue. There is nothing nearly as satisfying as stoking a hardwood fire and listening to meat sizzle. I hope as you read and learn from this book that you too will become a convert.

INTRODUCTION

Since you're reading this book, you probably have some sort of grill or smoker and you have tried with some success to cook mouthwatering barbecue. You may ask yourself, "What do I need to improve my barbecuing skills?" Many people think the answer is more expensive and bigger equipment. When I was visiting Alabama, I met a pit master who had the best barbecue I had ever tried. What was amazing to me is that his pit consisted of cinder blocks, an expanded metal grate, and steel flashing for a lid. He shoveled coals around and through split hardwood when needed. At this point I was relying on my equipment with all of the gadgets. I watched my thermometers like a hawk—both fore temperature and meat temperature. This old pit master told me, "No need for all that stuff. I let the fire tell me how hot it is and the meat tell me when it's ready to be turned or ready to be pulled." I asked him how he determined this, and he told me, "The barbecue sings to you. You just have to learn how to listen." I thought about what he told me and tried to understand what he meant by it. I tried to listen for the singing, but every time I would look at a thermometer my head would take over and I would follow the processes as I had learned them.

I thought back to my church mission when I was visiting the home of a blind family in one of the areas I was serving in. They had a piano, and I sat down and started playing a church hymn. Mrs. Sawyer told me to stop playing. I stopped and she said, "It's too mechanical. Let the piano sing the music to you as you play it. Now start again." I did so, and she stopped me once more. "Do you have the notes memorized?" I said I did. She told me, "Close your eyes and play it again, but this time let the piano sing to you as you play it." I did, and the piano sang! She jumped up and clapped. "That's exactly what I was talking about. It is beautiful." Then she said, "People who see miss so much because they rely too much on their eyes and not enough on the other senses."

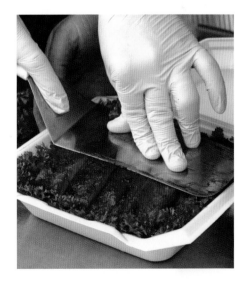

It made sense to me—the old pit master in Alabama, the sweet blind lady from my mission. There is so much more to barbecue than temperatures and processes. A love has to be put into the meat. When this love is applied, the meat will sing to you and tell you when it is done. It is a beautiful thing! In the months following, I took out my thermometers and cooked the meat. I noticed a huge difference immediately. I've kept this up, and it works better and better every time. I love listening to the crackle of a fire and the sizzle of the meat. When your heart and soul is put into the barbecue, the meat will respond in kind. People who try your food will think that you are a wizard!

In this book, everything I teach is designed to take away the hard learning curve that I had to go through. I will teach you the basics. It is important at first to learn the temperatures and processes. After you learn to use the equipment and the proper process to create great barbecue, using your other senses will take your barbecue to a different place.

1

BARBECUE BEGINNINGS

Barbecue has been around since the dawn of man. In its simplest form, it is meat cooked over wood coals. The word "barbecue" is thought to come from the Spanish word *barbacoa*, or the Caribbean word *barabicu*. "Barbacoa" means "fire pit." Traditional barbacoa is done by digging a pit, filling it with coals, and slow cooking a whole meat like a goat or a sheep. Barbecue as we know it today is an American food through and through. There are four main hubs of barbecue recognized in the United States: Carolina, Memphis, Texas, and Kansas City.

Carolina barbecue originated in the 1860s. After the slaves were emancipated, they moved North and settled in the woods of North Carolina and Tennessee. Wild pigs ranged across much of the South and were particularly thick in the mountains of North Carolina. The wild hogs had been brought to the continent with the European settlers. They flourished here and became a large feral population. The newly freed slaves exploited this source of meat. They dug large pits outside to cook since it was too hot to cook inside their homes. Hardwood was the available fuel source to cook the pork. They learned that if they cooked it low and slow, the otherwise tough meat became juicy and tender. The vinegar prevalent in their sauce was used to hide the slight taint the meat had after a few days without refrigeration.

Carolina-style barbecue is marked today by two subregions: Piedmont and Western. The main meat is pork, and a thin vinegar sauce is preferred. The Piedmont style is chopped fine, and all the meat is mixed together. Usually either the whole hog or the whole shoulder with skin on the pork is used. The Western style is more of a pulled pork, and a thicker tomato-based sauce is typically used.

Memphis barbecue had similar beginnings but is known for the pork ribs. This is thought to be because ribs were not a highly sought after piece of meat. People could buy the meat for very little and make it incredibly good by cooking it low and slow. Memphis is known for using rubs (mixtures of spices) on the ribs. In Memphis today you can order ribs dry or wet (with or without sauce).

Across the continent in the Wild West, cattlemen ran large herds of longhorn cattle across the arid deserts of what is now Texas. They slaughtered the longhorns on the trail as needed and slowly cooked the meat over mesquite wood coals, the only fuel source available. The normally tough longhorns and especially the brisket could be made incredibly tender and flavorful cooking over the mesquite coals.

About this same time, a city built around a rail spur started to boom. Word of the amazing meat reached Kansas City, and a new barbecue was developed. Kansas City gained popularity mixing all types of meats and techniques with a sweet tomato-based sauce. Kansas City has the argument of being the hub of all barbecue in the United States.

A couple other types of barbecue are noteworthy. Kentucky barbecue is known for its mutton. Santa Maria barbecue is known for cooking beef over an oak fire on an open pit with an adjustable cooking rack called a Santa Maria grill. Nowadays, with the popularity of barbecue, there is not a place in the United Stated that does not have its own variation of barbecue. But they all have one thing in common: slow-cooked meat on a wood fire. The propane industry pitches the slogan, "Taste the food and not the fuel." The whole idea of barbecue is to taste the fuel—every wood has a distinct flavor that enhances the natural flavors in the meat. Barbecue is primal; you get an intense satisfaction cooking over fire. I believe in a dormant barbecue gene that was passed to us from our ancestors—when we cook with fire, we wake up that gene, and the fire builds in our blood. It becomes an addiction. That is why people are so crazy about barbecue. Some recipe secrets are kept in safes and passed from generation to generation, and this is related just to the home cook. When barbecue becomes a revenue source, even more protection is employed by companies to keep the edge with their recipes and techniques. All the recipes in this book are simply a starting point. As you experiment and try things on your own, you will find what works best for you and hopefully develop a barbecue legacy of your own.

4

SMOKING, BARBECUING, AND GRILLING

Oftentimes, "smoking," "barbecuing," and "grilling" are used as if they are synonymous. The most common misuse is people saying they are barbecuing when they are actually grilling on a gas grill in their backyard. And many people will say they are smoking when they are barbecuing. There is a big difference between the three. The distinction, simply put, is temperature. Whether the heat source is direct or indirect does not matter.

SMOKING

Smoking is cooking at a temperature below 150 degrees. When you are smoking, you are generally not trying to cook but to cure instead. Smoking is used most often for fish, jerky, and cheeses. The smoke, in addition to adding flavor to whatever you are cooking, adds aldehydes, which make great food preservatives (in small amounts). You have to be careful, though, because too much aldehyde will make your food taste strong and your mouth numb or tingly as you eat it. Most often, smoking is done using an indirect heat method because the direct heat is too intense and will cook the food instead of curing it. When the food reaches temperatures above 150 degrees, the proteins change and the food has a different texture and taste. Smoking has been used for centuries as one of the best ways to preserve meat. At a recent church activity, I was in charge of the food for a pioneer trek re-creation. As part of the experience, I let the young adults make jerky the same way their pioneer ancestors did. We cut the meat into strips, soaked it in a brine, and hung it in the sun with smoke to dry. This is one of the food items they were able to take with them on the trail.

COOKING TEMPERATURES

Smoking .... below 150°F

Barbecuing ...200°F–300°F

Grilling.........above 300°F

Smoking today is not a necessity of life but rather for flavor. Many cheeses can be brought to a new level of flavor with the addition of smoke.

Fishing will bring a whole new excitement if you can produce amazing smoked fish. Jerky made in this manner is so much better than store–bought jerky or even home-made jerky using liquid smoke. In a future chapter, I describe how to set up a smoker and give you some recipes to try.

BARBECUING

Barbecuing is cooking at a temperature range of 200–300 degrees. "Low and slow," as many people say. Barbecuing can be done with direct heat from an outdoor grill or indirect heat with an offset smoker. A barbe-cue pit can range from an inexpensive fifty-gallon drum to a $15,000 trailer rig smoker. Almost any meat can be barbecued, though some work better than others. If there is a lack of fat and collagen in the meat, it cannot be cooked to 200 degrees without drying out. Adversely, meat with a lot of fat and collagen can be cooked to 200 degrees and be tender and moist. The most common meats to bar-becue are pork (whole or parts), beef brisket, ribs (pork or beef), chicken (thighs, halves, or whole), lamb, and turkey. Barbecue is con-sidered an art form, and many people don't try it because they are intimidated. In this book I will show you how simple it is—you'll become a pit master in no time.

GRILLING

Grilling is exclusively direct heat at tem-peratures above 300 degrees. Grilling is often mislabeled in American culture as bar-becuing. Grills range from small, charcoal, kettle-style grills to expensive infrared gas grills. Grilling is great for steaks, burgers, chicken, chops, and fish. Grilling offers a unique charred flavor where the rack meets the meat. The drippings from the meat burn in the flame and produce a pleasant flavor in the meat as well. Grilling is something that every man should learn to master and can in no time at all. In a later chapter, I teach you techniques and give you recipes that will help you to master the grill.

WOOD AND UNLEASHING THE FLAVOR

As previously stated, the propane slogan says, "Taste the food, not the fuel." But what if the fuel enhances the flavor of your food? There is nothing quite as good as a burger cooked on a charcoal grill or a steak cooked over a wood coal fire. Many restaurants now claim with pride "Wood fire–grilled." There is a reason—people like the taste of the wood. The propane folks probably douse their food in liquid smoke, which is amusing to me because they are putting imitation wood fuel flavor back into the food that they claimed they wanted to taste without the fuel. Wood smoke wakes up a flavor profile in food that hits to the core of our primitive genes. Our ancestors always cooked with wood, and I believe it wakes up that gene in all of us.

Using the right type of wood greatly affects the flavor of your food. You should always use a hard wood. Soft woods, such as pine and fir, have pitch in them, so when they cook, the pitch becomes a vapor and is absorbed into your meat. It will give your meat a turpentine taste. The only time you can use a soft wood for cooking is if it is burned completely to coals.

Understanding how charcoal is made is important, as is how it can affect your food. Charcoal is compressed wood chips that have been heated to the point of turning into char. They still have a lot of flavor left in them. Some of the most flavorful charcoals are made with mesquite and oak. The advantage of using charcoal is the consistent burn temperature.

The following list of woods are commonly used for smoking and barbecue. It is up to you to find what flavor profile you like.

HICKORY

Hickory is the most common wood used in barbecue nationwide. The smell of hickory-cooking meat is instantly recognizable to almost anyone. Hickory grows throughout much of the South and Southeast.

and it has a distinct flavor that is especially good with beef and pork. The smoke color from oak is deep and penetrates well. Oak is also used exclusively in Santa Maria–style barbecue of coastal California, where beef is the meat of choice. *(Pictured: Bottom right).*

CHERRY

Cherry has a fairly mild, sweet-flavored smoke, and it is particularly good on poultry. Extra caution should be taken to remove the bark since it has a lot of aldehydes that will give the meat a bitter flavor. *(Pictured: Bottom left).*

APPLE

Apple is the mildest of all the woods and is great on poultry and fish, where other woods can overpower the flavor of the meat. Like cherry, you should avoid burning the bark or small twigs because it will become bitter.

ALDER

Alder has a unique flavor that pairs best with oily fish, such as salmon and trout. It is the most common wood used to smoke fish and cheese. It has a nutty flavor that is fairly mild. *(Pictured: Top).*

MESQUITE

Mesquite is the second most common wood used in barbecue, though mostly in charcoal form. It is paired best with beef— mesquite smoke became famous on the long

Hickory smoke has a slightly pungent flavor but balances well with almost any meat; however, it should be used cautiously because it can overpower the meat. Oftentimes hickory is best if burnt to coals first before being presented to the pit to cook the meat.

PECAN

Pecan is used all across the South and has a similar flavor to hickory, but it is much milder. You use it in much the same way as hickory for all meat types. It has a slight peppery flavor.

OAK

Oak is my personal favorite. It is used exclusively throughout central and east Texas, cattle drives of south and west Texas. Mesquite in lump form should be used very sparingly because it is full of creosote and can ruin meat quickly. I recommend always using mesquite in a charcoal form, where it is most delicious.

PEACH

Peach wood is used a lot in Georgia for cooking pork. It is the sweetest of all the fruitwoods and has a nice flavor that will go well with most meats. It is one of the hardest woods to get ahold of because people don't like cutting down their peach trees. Like other fruitwoods, the bark should be removed.

PLUM AND APRICOT

Plum and apricot are very dense and heavy woods and will give you a great coal base to cook with, but they have little flavor. When using either of these woods, pair it with a different wood for flavor.

GRAPEVINES

Grapevines are becoming common in California to cook barbecue. This wood has a unique flavor, is somewhat strong, and is hard to get ahold of.

MAPLE

Maple has a strong flavor but creates a great coal base and can be paired with another wood for flavor. Sugar maples of the Northeast have the best flavor and go well with poultry.

There are many hardwoods that I have not listed. I wouldn't have enough room in the book to list them all. The above are simply the most common. A few important things to consider when trying out a wood: make sure the wood is dry and cured and the bark is removed, and try to burn it to coals before you put the meat on it. This way, if you are unsure about the wood, you won't ruin your meat. Don't be afraid to experiment and find out what combination of woods you like. If you are cooking on a charcoal grill, do not use match light–style charcoal because the petroleum base can penetrate your meat and make it taste like gasoline. If you are going to use match light, burn it outside of your pit until the charcoals are completely gray before putting them in your pit.

Popular Types of Charcoal for Barbecue

KINGSFORD (BLUE BAG) is far and away the most reliable and consistent burning charcoal. It is made of a combination of fir trees and alder from the sawmills in coastal Oregon. There is no pine flavor, but there is a mild alder flavor that flavors your food.

ROYAL OAK is the second most popular charcoal, made from oak trees. It has a pleasant flavor and a consistent burn. Royal oak is the choice charcoal of most pro-division barbecue teams.

MESQUITE LUMP CHARCOAL has the best flavor of all the charcoals but does not burn consistently and pops as it burns, so caution is needed when cooking—don't be near anything flammable. Unlike the other types of charcoal, mesquite lump is not in briquettes, but charred logs. It is used by a lot of restaurants and barbecue competitors. It is a favorite of Latin cooking and is available at most Latin markets.

TYPES OF BARBECUE PITS

Barbecue pits can range from a grate set on stones over an open fire pit to a $20,000 custom-built trailer rig. The most common pit is the everyday backyard grill. This can be charcoal or gas, and though its primary function is to grill, it can also be used to barbecue or smoke.

If you have a gas grill, place wood chips in a foil pouch (made by folding the foil in half and folding the ends—it should resemble a canoe). Leave a small opening in the top. Place the foil and chips on the flame distribution plate. If your gas grill has two sides of heat, only use the heat on the side with the foil and chips, and cook on the other side.

If you have a charcoal grill, dampen your heat and add the chips directly onto the coals. Be sure not to let the chips flare up because it may burn the meat. It may take a little practice, but your results will be amazing no matter what you are cooking.

The original barbecue pits were just that—pits dug into the earth and filled with hot coals. The meat was put on spits or woven racks, or covered in large leaves like bananas. Later, racks of steel were forged to set over coals in a fire pit. Today in the South, many modern versions of this type of pit are built of cinder blocks with expanded metal racks and steel flashing for a lid. The hardwood is burned to coals in an area separate from the pit. The hot coals are then shoveled into the bottom of the pit by the pitmaster, where they cook low and slow. This method of cooking has great results because a coal has more even heat and better taste than an open flame. Also there is no chance of aldehydes giving your meat a bitter flavor since they have burned out prior to being placed in the vicinity of the meat. It is not always practical to build such a pit in your backyard unless you entertain a lot and cook for large groups of people. The advantage of this type of pit is the amount of meat that can be cooked at

BIG GREEN EGG   DRUM SMOKER

PELLET SMOKER

WEBER SMOKEY MOUNTAIN COOKER

the same time. These types of pits can be used to cook whole hogs as well.

Another common and inexpensive pit is Weber Smokey Mountain Cooker, or WSM. This direct-heat-style smoker uses charcoal as its main heat source. There are many knock-offs, but the true WSM remains the most popular. For the price, the quality of barbecue on one of these pits is hard to beat. You can barbecue or smoke on one of these pits. Grilling, however, would be difficult since the fire and heat would be problematic to control with the lid open. One major advantage for barbecue is that you can set it and forget it. It maintains constant heat rather well. Be careful not to open the lid too often since the extra oxygen will cause the fire to flare up and get too hot quickly. The only downfall to barbecue is the amount of meat you are able to cook. It's fine if you're cooking for your family and maybe entertaining a small group, but a large amount of meat is simply not possible.

My favorite pit on a budget is a drum smoker. It is often called by many names: UDS (ugly drum smoker), BDS (big drum smoker), or a garbage can pit (many were built from metal garbage cans). The drum smoker uses a similar direct-heat process like the WSM to barbecue and smoke. A basket is placed in the bottom of a drum filled with unlit charcoal. You light the top layer and add wood chunks to the top. The bottom of the drum has holes that serve as air inlets and regulate the heat. The more air that enters in, the hotter the fire will be. As the fire burns down, it will ignite the charcoal below. A well-built drum smoker will maintain heat for twelve hours or more off one basket full of charcoal. The racks for cooking are placed in the top part of the drum and allow enough

OFFSET SMOKER

allowing you to choose the profile you want for what you are cooking. Pellet smokers are great for beginners to barbecue; they are easy to use and forgiving. The major disadvantage is the price. A good-quality pellet smoker can cost from several hundred dollars to over a thousand dollars. They come in many different sizes, from cooking for your own family to entertaining a large group or even catering.

Offset stick burners are my favorite types of pits. They are available in "direct-flow," meaning the fire and the exhaust are on opposite ends of the pit, and "reverse-flow," where the exhaust and the fire are on the same end of the pit. These pits use mainly wood logs for fuel, although many pitmasters use charcoal as a base for the fire. The fire in an offset should burn bright and hot, with the temperature controlled by the overall size of the pit and the offset cooking chamber. The major advantage of an offset pit is, bar none, the flavor. I don't believe you can have a better smoke flavor in any other type of pit. I cooked on drums and WSMs for years, and when I finally built my reverse-flow offset, I was amazed at the flavors I was able to achieve with my pit. An offset pit can range from a small porch model to a large trailer-style rig. The disadvantage of an offset smoker is the learning curve. An offset smoker can take years to master. The heat control is directly related to the type of wood you use and your fire-control techniques. You have to constantly watch the fire and make sure it stays lit or your food will not cook. The other disadvantage is that the wood needs to be in logs, not chips or chunks. But you can cook for large groups and even huge events, depending on your smoker, and the quality is unparalleled.

space for larger meats, such as pork shoulders. The lid of the drum also has holes that allow for the pit to breathe and the smoke to escape. The major advantage of a drum smoker is that you can have a great smoker built for less than a hundred dollars. Another advantage is the barbecue off a drum smoker is hard to beat. The drums are easy to clean as well—as the fat renders off the meat, it burns in the fire instead of collecting in the smoker. The disadvantage is similar to the WSM, but not as drastically—you cannot prepare a lot of meat at one time on a drum. Most people I know usually have three to four drums and end up cooking a lot of food on a number of them rather than opting for a more expensive pit.

Pellet smokers are becoming popular because of their ease of use. Pellets are fed into a small electricity-fed fire and produce a lot of smoke and heat to barbecue or smoke with. The advantages of the pellet smokers are consistent heat and flavor. An electric thermostat will feed the pellets at the exact rate needed to maintain temperature. The pellets come in many different flavors,

TYPES OF BARBECUE PITS

Another pit style that has become popular in recent years is the Santa Maria–style pit. Santa Maria pits were made famous by the cowboys of the Santa Maria region of California. The pits feature a flat fire rack that cooks with open flame under an adjustable rack cooking surface controlled by a cable and pulley system. The Santa Maria pits were traditionally used to cook beef over an oak fire, but they can be used to cook any type of barbecue with any wood. The cooking rack raises and lowers over the fire to adjust the temperature. This is an advantage in that you can cook everything from burgers to brisket. The other advantage of using a Santa Maria pit is a different taste of barbecue; the open flame will produce a different flavor in meat than will smoke cooking through an offset. Also, the direct fire will burn off any grease that drops, making this pit easy to clean. The disadvantage is that some high-fat meats will drip so much grease that the flame will flare up, and the pit will not rise up high enough to avoid charring the meat as you cook. For this reason a lot of people stick with cooking beef on a Santa Maria pit.

To combat this problem, there is another pit designed from the Santa Maria pit and made popular in South America—the Argentine grill. The only difference between the Santa Maria pit and the Argentine grill is the cooking rack. The Argentine grill uses an inverted angle iron (with the angle sitting as a "V" shape and the cooking surface on top of the "V"). The angle irons are placed close together with less than an inch of space between each one. The cooking rack is slightly beveled to one side. The advantages to this cooking rack are that the angle iron will heat up and disperse the heat more evenly to avoid charring the meat, and the angle iron acts as a trough for the dripping fat, which runs through the angle iron to a fat collection basin on one side of the pit. The disadvantages are few. Most people think it is a better design, but some think that a little of the open flame flavors are lost due to the tight space of the angles as opposed to the open expanded metal of the Santa Maria–style pit. Both of these pits come in a number of size options—from small backyard models on wheels to large trailer-pull models for catering events to permanent stone-built pits in restaurants and some backyards.

The Internet—particularly online barbecue forums—is a great resource for finding diagrams on each type of pit and how it works.

FIRE CONTROL

F ire control is the single most important element in good barbecue. If the temperature is too high, your meat will cook too fast and dry out. If the temperature is too low, you will have a smoky, smudgy fire that will give an off flavor to your meat.

Many elements can affect your fire: humidity, barometric pressure, type of wood, wind, and so on. To become a true pitmaster, you need to learn how to adapt and work with all of these conditions. This is the reason so many people start off with a pellet cooker or something similar—they are so much easier to control.

A lot of tricks can help you out along the way. Charcoal is one of your greatest assets in controlling a fire. Charcoal burns hot and even and allows you a baseline to begin cooking. You can add wood a little at a time for the flavor and to replace the coals being burnt. One method of using charcoal is to fill a basket in your firebox with unlit charcoal. Light the top layer of charcoal and place your wood on top of that. The unlit charcoal will burn a layer at a time and keep a consistent layer of heat in your pit. Add logs a little at a time for flavor and you will have a good barbecue product. For purists, charcoal does not fit within their vernacular; they want to cook with pure wood. This is fine, but you just need to create a base layer of heat and coals. One technique I have used is the log cabin method. For this I use four logs of equal size. I put two parallel logs on the bottom with a log's width in between. I stack the other logs on top in the opposite direction. I use a torch to light my fire and get the wood burning well. As the fire burns, the coals will build up and create a base layer. Every hour and a half to two hours I add four more logs in the same manner. This keeps the consistency and the flavor I need for great barbecue.

Wind is the single hardest element to deal with in maintaining a good fire. To understand why, you need to understand the Venturi principal: the fast-moving air blowing across the top of your smoke stack will create a vacuum and suck all of the smoke and heat out of your pit. The same thing will happen to the baffles on your firebox. This is quite difficult to deal with and will frustrate most pitmasters until they

learn to deal with the wind. For the smoke stack, if you have a baffle on top, this is the one time you want to keep the baffle closed off. If you do not have a baffle, you can invest in a 90-degree elbow that you can turn away from the wind. This will help most of the time. For the firebox, you need to close off as many vents as you can and still allow a flame to burn. If you can, build a movable wind wall out of some wood fence panels to stop the wind from blowing across your firebox.

The color of your smoke is an important indicator of how your fire is burning. Smoke means one thing: your fire is not burning well. A clean-burning fire will produce little to no smoke. The smoke coming out of your stack should be bright white to blue and very thin. If the smoke is heavy and billowing, your fire is not burning well. If you see brown or yellow smoke, remove whatever wood you were using and start over immediately. There is no such thing as good barbecue off a smoker that is putting out brown or yellow smoke.

A simple rule of thumb with fire control: The more air allowed into the fire, the hotter it will be. You need to be careful when using a drum or WSM-style pit because when you lift the lid, you introduce oxygen and the fire will become extremely hot. I have seen drums go from 250 degrees to 750 degrees in a matter of a couple of minutes. Don't let this scare you away—with a little practice and a little patience you will have it down in no time. Remember, practice makes perfect, and your family and friends will love your practice.

SMOKING RECIPES AND TECHNIQUES

Smoking is cooking at a temperature lower than 150 degrees. The idea is not to cook the food but to preserve the food using smoke. Some examples of smoked foods are jerky, smoked fish, smoked cheese, and cold sausages (such as summer sausage). The hardest part about smoking is keeping the temperature low. Often this is accomplished by having the fire completely separate from the smoke chamber. In the 1800s, almost every farm had a smokehouse where they would hang meats cured in salt to preserve them. These smokehouses were anywhere from ten feet by ten feet to even larger depending on how much meat needed to be cured. The fire would be made outside the smokehouse, usually in a below-ground level pit. The smoke would travel through a tunnel and into the smokehouse. A lot of these types of smokehouses still exist in the Appalachian mountains and Alaska but are sadly gone from most everywhere else. Still, you certainly do not need to build this type of smokehouse to enjoy smoked meat.

If you have an offset smoker, smoking will be easy—simply keep your fire small. The easiest way is with a small commercial smoker such as a Camp Chef smoke vault or a Little Chief smoker. These smokers are small and easy to smoke with a low temperature. A lot of these types of smokers will have an electricity-controlled thermostat that will maintain an even temperature. The hardest smokers to smoke on are the drum or WSM-style smokers. It can be done, but with the direct heat, keeping them from getting too hot is difficult. If you want, you can use your propane backyard grill to smoke meats. Turn one side's temperature to as low as it will go. Place a foil pouch of water-soaked wood chips on the heating element. Put your food on the top rack opposite of the side the wood chips are on. For best results, crack the lid of the grill open as you smoke.

SMOKED FISH

A lot of people love to eat smoked fish but don't know how to make it. They end up spending a lot of money on something they can easily do at home. Any fish can be smoked, but fish with a high-fat content absorb the smoke better. The most common types of fish to smoke are salmon, trout, mackerel, and herring. These fish are fairly oily and stay nice when smoked. Whitefish such as halibut and catfish will require a considerable brine to turn out good. Two distinct methods are used to smoke fish: the lox method and the hot smoke method.

LOX METHOD

The lox, or cold, method originates from Scandinavia and Northern Europe. In Ireland, it is known as lox. Salmon is the number one fish to prepare in this way. The lox will finish very moist and a little salty. The meat will appear slightly translucent and raw, though the colors will be intensified. To make lox, you need to soak the skinless fillets in a brine for up to twenty days. This will completely cure the meat and preserve it.

LOX

BASIC BRINE:

1 gallon cold water

1 cup kosher salt

1 cup sugar

3–5 lbs. boneless, skinless salmon or trout

black pepper

Make the basic brine and soak the salmon fillets in the brine in the refrigerator for 10–20 days. Rinse off the fillets and let them sit on a drip rack until the outside is starting to dry a little. Sprinkle with black pepper. Smoke the fillets in a pit at 85–100 degrees using alder wood for 3–5 hours. When the lox is done, the meat will be slightly transparent and all the same color. Wrap the lox in plastic wrap or vacuum-seal them and freeze to store. Lox are a great addition to sushi rolls or fresh spring rolls, or served on a sandwich or bagel with cream cheese.

HOT SMOKED FISH

The natives of Alaska have been smoking salmon to preserve it since the dawn of their civilization. The traditional way of preservation was to cut the fillets into strips with the skin on and hang them to dry with alder wood smoke. This technique is still being used today. I like to use flavored brines and rubs to add a little extra flavor to my fish. Here are some recipes.

CAJUN-STYLE SMOKED FISH

BASIC BRINE:

1 gallon cold water

1 cup kosher salt

1 cup sugar

¼ cup Tony Chachere's cajun seasoning

½ cup cider vinegar

1 large onion, peeled but left whole

3–5 lbs. fish fillets (skin on), cut into strips

Mix the brine, cajun seasoning, cider vinegar, and onion together. Add the fish fillets. Soak them for 1–3 days. Smoke over alder wood or applewood at 135 degrees for 7–8 hours, or until it is dried to your desired doneness level. The fish should be solid in color. Let the fillets relax until they are at room temperature. Wrap in plastic or vacuum-seal them and freeze to keep fresh.

COLA SMOKED FISH

Basic Brine (see recipe above)

1 (2-liter) bottle cola

¼ cup black pepper

3–5 lbs. fish fillets, skin on

Mix the brine, cola, and black pepper together. Soak the fish fillets in the brine for 1–3 days. Cook over alder wood at 135 degrees for 10–12 hours. Let the fillets relax to room temperature. Wrap in plastic wrap or vacuum-seal them and freeze to keep fresh.

TERIYAKI-STYLE SMOKED FISH

BASIC BRINE:

1 gallon cold water

1 cup kosher salt

1 cup sugar

1 cup soy sauce

1 can crushed pineapple

1 cup brown sugar

1 Tbsp. ginger

¼ cup black pepper

3–5 pounds of skin-on
fish fillets

Mix the brine, soy sauce, crushed pineapple, brown sugar, ginger, and black pepper together. Add the fish fillets. Soak them for 1–3 days. Smoke over alder wood or applewood at 135 degrees for 7–8 hours, or until it is dried to your desired doneness level. The fish should be solid in color. Let the fillets relax until they are at room temperature. Wrap in plastic or vacuum-seal them and freeze to keep fresh.

TRADITIONAL SMOKED SALMON

BASIC BRINE:

1 gallon cold water

1 cup kosher salt

1 cup sugar

3–5 lbs. fish fillets, skin on

Soak the fish fillets in the brine for 1–3 days. Cook over alder wood at 135 degrees for 10–12 hours. Let the fillets relax to room temperature. Wrap in plastic wrap or vacuum-seal them and freeze to keep fresh.

JERKY

For years, people have asked me when I was going to do a book about jerky. When I was young, my dad always made deer jerky whenever he got a deer. We loved the jerky; it was our candy. We would sneak jerky out of the freezer, hoping my dad would not notice. Still to this day, when I smell his jerky being dried, I start to get excited. The cool thing about jerky is there are no limits. You can play with recipes and experiment. If you find exactly what you like, write it down for your own jerky recipe.

Originally jerky was made simply by drying the meat out. Drying meat out over smoke added flavor and preserved the meat for longer. Rock salt was added and jerky became a mainstay. Meat was easy to preserve and had great flavor, and jerky could be reconstituted and used to make other meals. Jerky can be made out of any type of meat. Beef, pork, and game are the most common, but fowl can be used as well. To make jerky, cut the slabs as evenly as possible between ⅛ and ¼ inch thick. Cut the jerky along the grain of the meat, rather than against it. Otherwise the jerky will fall apart.

TRADITIONAL JERKY

3–5 lbs. meat

1 gallon water

1 cup salt

Cut the meat into strips with the grain of the meat. Soak the meat for 1–3 days in the water and salt. Smoke the meat at 135 degrees over any type of hardwood for several hours until it reaches desired doneness. Try different woods for different flavors.

OLD-FASHIONED JERKY

3–5 lbs. meat

½ gallon water

½ gallon apple juice

1 cup kosher salt

1 cup brown sugar

¼ cup black pepper

½ cup Worcestershire sauce

Cut the meat into strips with the grain of the meat. Combine the water, apple juice, kosher salt, brown sugar, black pepper, and Worcestershire sauce. Soak the meat in this mixture for 1–3 days. Smoke the meat at 135 degrees over any type of hardwood for several hours until it reaches desired doneness. Try different woods for different flavors.

TERIYAKI JERKY

3–5 lbs. meat

½ gallon water

2 cups soy sauce

1 cup crushed pineapple

1 cup brown sugar

1 Tbsp. ginger

Cut the meat into strips with the grain of the meat. Combine the water, soy sauce, pineapple, brown sugar, and ginger. Soak the meat in this mixture for 1–3 days. Smoke the meat at 135 degrees over any type of hardwood for several hours until it reaches desired doneness. Try different woods for different flavors.

DAD'S JERKY

3–5 lbs. meat

4 cups water

2 cups soy sauce

1 cup Worcestershire sauce

½ cup brown sugar

2 Tbsp. black pepper

1 tsp. cayenne pepper

1 can cola

Cut the meat into strips with the grain of the meat. Combine the water, soy sauce, Worcestershire sauce, brown sugar, black pepper, cayenne pepper, and cola. Soak the meat in this mixture for 1–3 days. Smoke the meat at 135 degrees over any type of hardwood for several hours until it reaches desired doneness. Try different woods for different flavors.

BLACK PEPPER JERKY

3–5 lbs. meat

½ gallon water

¼ cup kosher salt

½ cup soy sauce

½ cup Worcestershire sauce

½ cup black pepper

½ cup brown sugar

Cut the meat into strips with the grain of the meat. Combine the water, kosher salt, soy sauce, Worcestershire sauce, black pepper, and brown sugar. Soak the meat in this mixture for 1–3 days. Smoke the meat at 135 degrees over any type of hardwood for several hours until it reaches desired doneness. Try different woods for different flavors.

SWEET BARBECUE JERKY

3–5 lbs. meat

½ gallon water

½ cup Worcestershire sauce

1 cup barbecue sauce

½ cup brown sugar

2 Tbsp. black pepper

2 Tbsp. kosher salt

Cut the meat into strips with the grain of the meat. Combine the water, Worcestershire sauce, barbecue sauce, brown sugar, black pepper, and kosher salt. Soak the meat for 1–3 days. Smoke the meat at 135 degrees over any type of hardwood for several hours until it reaches desired doneness. Try different woods for different flavors.

HAM, BACON, AND TURKEY

Hams and bacons have been made for hundreds of years. The process of making a ham involves completely curing the meat with salt. The difference between brining and curing is the amount of time you leave meat in the brine. When you brine meat, the salt preserves the outside membrane of the cell. So when you cook the meat, the preserved cell membrane does not allow the moisture to evaporate as quickly. However, when you cure the meat, you preserve the entire cell, and the composition of the meat changes. The traditional method of curing hams and bacons is to pack them in rock salt. This method is now referred to as country-style ham and country-style bacon. These are the hams you would see hanging in a meat shop with a coated white layer. Spain specializes in the aging and curing of hams known as serrano ham. In Italy, the hams from black-footed hogs raised on acorns are cured into prosciutto, which has a delicate flavor and takes a minimum of one year in perfect conditions to make. The country-style hams in the United States have great flavor but aren't aged to the extent of their European cousins. In Italy, bacons are also cured and aged as pancetta. The primary difference between the old-style or country-style hams and bacons verses modern day is that the modern-day hams and bacons are cooked whereas the country-style hams and bacons are salt cured and aged without being cooked.

VIRGINIA HAM

If you are visiting the Virginias, you are likely to encounter a Virginia-style ham. These hams have been made in this part of the country since the 1600s. They have a tender and unique taste. Before starting on an adventure to cure a Virginia ham, make sure that the outside temperature is holding between forty-five and sixty degrees. This occurs during the early spring or the late fall in most areas of the country. If you have an old root cellar, that will work great too since they generally stay at fifty degrees year-round. The ham will take close to sixty days to cure and age properly, but the results are worth the time.

4 lbs. rock salt

1 lb. brown sugar

4 oz. pink salt
(sodium nitrite)

1 fresh ham

To begin, mix the rock salt, brown sugar, and pink salt together and divide the mixture in half. Set one half aside for later. On a large baking sheet, lay the ham down and rub the other half of the salt mixture in well, making sure that you pack it in anywhere you can. Let the ham rest for an hour and repack it until you have used up all of the first half of salt mixture. Set the ham on a wire rack or hang it in a root cellar or outside where it is allowed to breathe. Let it sit for 7 days. After 7 days, break the crust off and repack it with the remaining salt you set aside originally. Hang the meat for another 7–14 days. Break the crust off again. Scrub the meat with a new plastic brush and water until no salt remains. Let the ham sit in a bath of cold water for several hours, changing the water out a couple of times. Prepare to smoke the meat using hardwood over low heat, about 135 degrees. This works best in a smokehouse or an offset pit. Smoke the ham for 5 hours or until the outside is a chestnut brown. When you are done smoking the ham, hang it back up in your root cellar and let it age for up to 45 days. The longer you age it, the more tender the meat will be and the stronger the flavor. When it is time to prepare the ham for a meal, let it sit in a water bath overnight. Rinse off the ham well and pat it dry. Bake the ham in the oven or smoker at 350 degrees for 5–7 hours with your favorite ham glaze.

COUNTRY-STYLE BACON

Country-style bacon is my favorite. I like to keep the slabs whole in my fridge so I can pull them out when I want bacon, and then I slice them thick and fry them up. Nothing beats the taste of bacon you cured yourself. This method is similar to the Virginia ham but without the aging. And country-style bacon is generally a little saltier and the pork flavor is more intense.

1 lb. kosher salt

½ lb. sugar

1 oz. pink salt (sodium nitrite)

2 pork bellies cut into 12-inch square slabs (or whatever size makes them even)

Mix the kosher salt, sugar, and pink salt together. Rub the salt mixture evenly onto the bacon slabs. Place the slabs on a rack in your fridge where they're okay to drip. Turn the slabs daily and cure them for 5–7 days. Break the salt crust free and rinse off the slabs thoroughly. Let them sit in a water bath to relax the slabs for several hours, changing the water out every hour. To test the saltiness, slice off a small piece of the bacon and fry it in a pan. If it is too salty, let it sit for a while longer before smoking it. When your bacon is ready to smoke, put it on a cool smoker at 135 degrees. Smoke it for 3–5 hours depending on the smoke taste desired. Let the bacon relax. Wrap it and let it age in the fridge for at least 1 week before cooking to eat. Cook it like any other type of bacon.

MODERN HAM

As mentioned before, the biggest difference between the modern hams and the Virginia hams is that the modern hams are cooked fully. The second difference is that the modern hams are also cured in a brine solution rather than dry cured.

2 gallons water

2 cups kosher salt

2 cups sugar

4 oz. pink salt
(sodium nitrite)

¼ cup seasonings of
your choice, such as
black pepper, mustard
seed, celery seed,
etc. (feel free to play
around with flavors)

1 fresh ham

To prepare the modern ham, you have several options. You can use a fridge, as long as it is large enough for a 5-gallon bucket. A cooler will work as well. Or, if it is cold enough outside (30–40 degrees), you can cure it outside. Another option is to cut the ham into smaller pieces and have several smaller hams. Mix together the water, kosher salt, sugar, pink salt, and seasonings of choice in a 5-gallon bucket, making sure the salt and sugar are completely dissolved. Place the ham in the bucket and place weight on top to make sure that it is totally submersed. If you need to, you can add water to make sure that it is covered. Age the ham in the bucket for 21 days in a cooler or fridge. Remove the ham from the bucket and let it drip dry for an hour before smoking it. Place the ham on a smoker, cooking around 200 degrees.

Smoke it for 3–5 hours. The internal temperature should reach 150–160 degrees. Remove the ham and let it relax to an ambient temperature. The ham is now ready to eat, or store it for a later time.

CANADIAN BACON

Canadian bacon is prepared in the exact same manner as the modern ham but is made from the tenderloins of the pig.

1 gallon water

1 cup kosher salt

1 cup brown sugar

2 oz. pink salt
(sodium nitrite)

2 Tbsp. black pepper

6 pork tenderloins
(not whole loins)

Mix the water, kosher salt, brown sugar, pink salt, and black pepper together in a large bowl. Place up to 2 tenderloins in a gallon-size ziplock bag. Do this for all 6 tenderloins. Cover the bags completely with brine. Let them cure in the fridge for seven to ten days. Remove them from the bags, let them drip dry, place them on your smoker at 180 degrees, and smoke them for 2–3 hours. The internal temperature should reach 150 degrees. They need to relax for 2 hours at room temperature, before wrapping and refrigerating.

BLACK PEPPER BACON

1 gallon water

1 cup kosher salt

1 cup brown sugar

¼ cup black pepper

2 oz. pink salt (sodium nitrite)

2 pork bellies

Mix the water, kosher salt, brown sugar, black pepper, and pink salt together, making sure the salt and sugar are completely dissolved. Cut the bellies into square chunks and set them in the brine. Brine the slabs for 5–7 days. Let them drip dry on a rack for about 1 hour before putting them in a smoker at 200 degrees for about 3 hours. The internal temperature should read 150 degrees when finished. Let the meat relax to an ambient temperature before slicing or storing.

MAPLE-CURED BACON

It is amazing to me the amount of money people spend on home bacon kits to create gourmet bacon. It is so easy to do yourself. This is one of my favorite ways to make bacon at home.

1 gallon water

1 cup kosher salt

1 cup maple sugar or
   2 cups maple syrup

2 oz. pink salt
   (sodium nitrite)

2 pork bellies

Mix the water, kosher salt, maple sugar or syrup, and pink salt together, making sure the salt and sugar are completely dissolved. Cut the pork bellies into square chunks and set them in the brine. Brine the slabs for 5–7 days. Let them drip dry on a rack for about 1 hour before putting them in a smoker at 200 degrees for about 3 hours. The internal temperature should read 150 degrees when finished. Let the meat relax to an ambient temperature before slicing or storing.

31

TURKEY HAM
(SMOKED TURKEY BREAST)

1 fresh, boneless,
   skinless turkey breast

1 gallon water

1 cup kosher salt

1 cup brown sugar

2 oz. pink salt
   (sodium nitrite)

2 Tbsp. black pepper

Generally the boneless skinless turkey breast is used so that it can be sliced into sandwich meat. As with the Canadian bacon, because the meat is smaller and there are no bones, you only need to cure the breast for 7 days in the brine solution (water, kosher salt, brown sugar, pink salt, and black pepper), and I smoke it at a lower temperature (about 180 degrees) to ensure I get enough smoke flavor into the meat. Cook for 3–5 hours. Also make sure to bring the turkey hams up to 165 degrees instead of 150 degrees internal temperature. A lot of people like to add black pepper to the brine and rub the outside of the breast with black pepper before they smoke it.

SMOKED CHEESE

There is no secret recipe for smoked cheese. Any semi-hard cheese without a rind can be smoked. Some examples are cheddar (mild works best), havarti, gouda, swiss, and gruyère. The trick is smoking it at a lower temperature. A pit above 100 degrees will melt the cheese instead of smoking it. This is difficult to do without an offset smoker. To smoke your cheese, heat your smoker to 80 degrees, place the cheese on the smoker, and smoke for 1–2 hours, rotating every 15 minutes. If the cheese is becoming too soft, remove it from the smoker and let it harden before returning to the smoker. If the cheese begins to weep, it will lose oils, causing you to have a dry and crumbly cheese. Throughout the process, gently squeeze the cheese. It should feel slightly soft but retain its shape.

BARBECUE RECIPES AND TECHNIQUES

7

Everybody loves the magic of great barbecue, but few know how to do it. Ultimately, the people who know how to create good barbecue are seen as magicians, able to take a cheap cut of meat and turn it into a mouthwatering, juicy, and tender meal. Most barbecue is learned by trial and error, and many people who have learned the secrets guard them jealously. The mark of great barbecue is meat that is tender, with a good balance of smoke, spice, sauce, and meat flavor. This delicate balance is hard to reach at first, but with practice, you will be able to achieve it fairly quickly.

PORK

Pork is the basis and the starting point of most barbecue. It is also the easiest to begin with. Three main cuts of hog are used for barbecue: whole hog, pork shoulder, and ribs.

WHOLE HOG

Whole hog has many challenges because parts of it tend to dry out, like the loins and ribs. The hams always take a lot more time to cook than the rest of the pig. Because of this challenge, whole hog is considered a pinnacle of barbecue perfection. The optimum size of a whole hog to cook is 80–110 pounds. Most meat cutters will be able to provide you with a whole hog with some advance notice. To prepare the whole hog, the first thing to do is inject the meat with an injection (see page 38). This allows the meat to take on a brine texture and flavor without having to brine the hog. Next, rub the hog with a barbecue rub, making sure the rub does not have too much sugar since the amount of time the hog takes to cook makes the sugar burn.

You'll also need a frame for the hog. The most common frame is made out of chicken wire, which allows you to turn and rotate the hog as it cooks and take it out of the pit. Most times, the hog will be cooked belly up, which allows the juices to cool and keep the meat moist. In the Polynesian islands and the Caribbean, a true pit is used to barbecue hogs. They dig a large pit three feet deep, six feet long, and three feet wide. In preparing to cook the hog, they light large fires in the pit and create a massive bed of coals in the bottom. Then they layer the bottom of the pit with banana leaves on top of wood. They lower the hog in the wire frame onto the banana leaves and then cover the top with more banana leaves. They roast the whole hog for up to sixteen hours, after which they remove a perfectly cooked hog.

One way of doing this is building an above-ground temporary pit out of cinder blocks, expanded metal, and steel flashing. You can build an amazing whole hog pit for less than a hundred dollars. Stack the cinder blocks in a six by three rectangle, leaving an opening at the bottom. After three rows of cinder blocks, lay the expanded metal (cut to size), and then stack two more rows of cinder blocks. Lay the flashing on top. In preparation to cooking, lay a base of charcoal across the entire bottom of the pit, several inches deep. Light some charcoal to place on the top and set hardwood logs in the bottom. Allow the fire to start and get a good base of coals hot. Once the fire is going, close off the opening at the bottom of your pit using steel flashing or blocks. Lower the hog in its wire frame onto the expanded metal rack and then cover it with the flashing. Cook it for eight to ten hours, rotating it every couple of hours

and adding wood to the fire. After the eight hours, wrap the hog in foil and continue cooking until a probe inserted into the ham near the bone reads 195 degrees. Let the hog relax for at least thirty minutes prior to serving it.

The second way of barbecuing a whole hog is with an offset pit. To do this, you will need an offset pit designed to specifically cook whole hogs. The opening has to be large enough that you can put the whole hog in the pit and rotate it. The cooking chamber should be a minimum of five feet long by two feet wide. This will accommodate a one hundred–pound hog. The skin of a hog cooked in an offset cooker will become extremely hard and deep chestnut in color. The skin will hold in all the moisture and juices, and, in my opinion, this the best way to cook a whole hog. A whole hog should take between twelve and sixteen hours to cook completely, so make sure you have ample time set aside before you tackle this feat.

The third way to cook a whole hog, which is very popular in the Philippines, is to cook it on a spit. Generally, small suckling hogs (between fifty and seventy pounds) are cooked with this method. The suckling hog is placed on a hand-turned spit, filled with herbs and fruit, and then stitched up the middle and cooked on the spit for up to eight hours over a bed of hot coals. The result is amazing but labor-intensive.

The beauty of cooking a whole hog is there are so many different types and textures of meat. From the white meat of the loins to the fatty dark meat of the jowls, you get the whole experience of eating pork. The presentation of a whole hog, barbecued chestnut red, always stirs an appetite.

WHOLE HOG INJECTION

½ gallon apple juice

3 cups cider vinegar

¼ cup barbecue rub (ground fine to be able to be injected) (see rubs starting on page 69)

¼ cup kosher salt

Mix the ingredients together until the salt is dissolved. Inject the muscles of the hog, especially the loins and hams. Let it sit with the injection for 3–5 hours before placing the hog on your pit.

PORK SHOULDER

Pork shoulders are sold as either whole shoulders or Boston butt roasts, referred to as pork butts. Pork butts are the most common meat used in barbecue. It is considered a low-end cut of meat because of the high-fat content and large amount of collagen, which make the meat extremely tough and undesirable unless it is barbecued. But that high-fat content and collagen is what makes it so good for barbecue. It helps to think of the collagen as pasta: if it's not cooked enough, it is hard and difficult to eat; once it has been cooked properly, it is tender and nice and holds moisture and flavor. And like pasta, if pork butt is overcooked, it becomes mushy and falls apart.

To prepare pork shoulder, use a barbecue rub with low to moderate sugar content (see the pork rub recipe on page 71). Make sure to cover it completely with the rub so the meat is not visible underneath. Let the pork stand until the rub appears moist. Heat up a smoker to 250–275 degrees. If you're using a direct-heat smoker, such as a WSM or drum-type, lay the pork butt fat side down to protect the meat from overcooking. If you are using an offset-type smoker, it doesn't matter which side is up. Cook the pork for 4–6 hours. The internal temperature should read between 130 and 150 degrees. Wrap the pork in two layers of heavy-duty aluminum foil. It is not necessary to wrap the pork, but most people do because it cooks slightly faster. Some people like to put them in a disposable foil pan to keep from losing the juices. Cook the pork for another 2–6 hours, until the internal temperature reaches 195–205 degrees. Do NOT let it cook any more than this or it will become mushy in texture. Pork will not absorb any more smoke after 150 degrees, so the outside can become too dark and crusty if not wrapped. If this is your desired result, then don't wrap the pork. As soon as you pull out the pork, open the foil and let it breathe for 15 minutes. The texture and flavor is best if you allow it to rest for at least 1 hour before pulling it.

There is no right or wrong way to pull the pork. Many tools are available on the market that can make this process fast, such as Bear Paws. I like to use my hands to pull pork. There are a few steps to pulling pork. First, remove the bone. The bone should pull fairly easily from the meat. Second, separate individual muscle groups. (Nine muscles make up the pork butt.) This will allow the meat to cool down quicker and make it easier to pull. Remove all the fat left and discard. The scent gland also needs to be discarded. Nobody wants to bite into a glob of fat when they are eating pulled pork. Once the muscles are separated, sprinkle the pork with a finish rub (generally with a higher sugar content and less salt), add a small amount of sauce, and then pull the muscles apart using your hands, Bear Paws, or a fork. Taste it and make sure that the flavor is where you want it. If you need to add more sauce or rub, do so, but gently fold it into the pork since your pork can become mushy by pulling it too much.

ST. LOUIS–STYLE RIBS

Ribs, like pork shoulder, became a popular barbecue item because they were originally an undesirable cut of meat. Ribs were made popular in Tennessee, which is considered the barbecue rib capital of the world. Not very many stores offer a St. Louis–cut rib. They are generally sold as whole spare ribs, which contain two parts: the rib tip and the St. Louis rib. To cut a St. Louis rib, lay the ribs flat, bone side down. Locate the longest rib bone and cut a straight line from the longest rib bone across the ribs, separating the rib tips from the rest. The St. Louis ribs should be square on both sides. Turn the ribs over and fillet off the flap of muscle still connected to the ribs. Remove the membrane from the inside of the ribs using a dull knife and a paper towel to get grip. Put a rub on both sides of the ribs, but not as heavily as with the pork—you should still be able to see meat under the rub. This rub can have a higher sugar content because of the relatively short cook time. Let the ribs relax with the rub for at least 30 minutes prior to cooking.

A lot of people use the 3-2-1 method of cooking St. Louis ribs: 3 hours on the smoke, bone side down; 2 hours wrapped in foil, bone side up; and 1 hour back on the smoke, with sauce, bone side down. This is a good starting point that will give you tasty, well-cooked ribs. Cook ribs at a slightly higher temperature than pork butts, about 275 degrees. If you do not wrap your ribs, you will need to mop them with a mop sauce (one-to-one mixture of cider vinegar and apple juice) or the ribs will dry out. Mop the ribs every half hour until done. Unwrapped ribs require the same amount of cook time, which is about 6 hours. When you probe the ribs with a meat thermometer, the probe should go through easily and the temperature should be between 195 and 205 degrees. Let the ribs relax for 15 minutes before cutting.

Ribs can be cooked quite well on an outdoor grill. Follow similar cooking methods above with your grill turned on very low. Using a mop sauce is a must when cooking with direct heat. A lot of times, people will add apple juice and brown sugar to the foil when they wrap their ribs. This will give it a nice sweet flavor on the outside of the ribs. St. Louis–style ribs are considered more difficult to cook than baby back ribs, so a lot of pitmasters choose to cook St. Louis–style in a competition setting to show off their prowess in cooking barbecue.

Rib tips are also great as a barbecue item, but they require a lot more time to cook than the St. Louis ribs. I like to cook rib tips for 3 hours on the smoke and 3 hours wrapped in foil and then 1 hour with a sauce in a half pan. Rib tips have a tremendous amount of flavor but a lot of cartilage. They make an excellent addition to baked beans, with a nice flavor and texture. Barbecue restaurants love rib tips because they make extra money by selling the tips and the St. Louis ribs.

BABY BACK RIBS

Baby back ribs have become a cult favorite since the 90s, with the restaurant chain Chili's singing the lyrics in their jingle, "Chili's baby back ribs." Baby back ribs, or loin back ribs, are cut from the highest portion of the rib cage right below the loins. They have a lot more curve to the bone, they are smaller than St. Louis ribs (thus the term "baby" back ribs), and they have much less fat than the St. Louis. The lack of fat in comparison gives baby back ribs the appeal to people who want to eat ribs but don't like the fat. The lack of fat also causes challenges in the cooking process—baby backs will generally cook a lot faster than St. Louis ribs and are much easier to overcook, resulting in dry ribs.

However, a few tricks will help you cook baby back ribs perfectly every time. To prepare them, first remove the membrane from the inside of the ribs by inserting a knife between the clear membrane and the rib bones. This is a lot easier toward the large end of the ribs. Work a pocket between the membrane and the bone big enough that you can grab hold of it. Using a paper towel, gently pull the membrane off the bones without tearing it. If you cook it with the membrane on, no smoke or flavor will penetrate through the membrane into the meat; also the membrane becomes tough and chewy. Because of the lack of fat in the ribs, I like to coat them with a small amount of oil to allow the rub to adhere to the ribs. Some people use mustard, which works as well, but I don't want the taste of the mustard on my ribs. Sprinkle the rub (see chapter 8) on lightly enough that you can still see the meat through the rub. Let the ribs stand for 15–20 minutes until the rub is moist on the ribs.

Place the ribs bone side down on the smoker set at 275 degrees. Cook the ribs for 2 hours on the smoke without touching them. Then place the ribs on some foil bone side up, create a basin in the foil, and cover the ribs with brown sugar, honey, or agave syrup. Also pour a little apple juice in the bottom of the foil. Carefully wrap the ribs and then wrap them again, making sure that nothing will leak out. Cook the ribs for 1–1½ hours more. Check for doneness by inserting a thermometer between the bones. The probe should go through easily (internal temperature should read 195 degrees). If the ribs are still tough, cook for 30 minutes longer and try again. Once they are done, open the ribs and let them relax for a few minutes. Return the ribs to the smoke, bone side down, and glaze them with your favorite sauce. Cook for 20 minutes until the sauce is setting up a little. Let the ribs relax for 10 minutes or so before cutting and eating.

FRESH BRATWURST

There is no end to the sausages you can make using pork. You can experiment with your own ideas and add any ingredients that you want. I have decided on the bratwurst because it is the most versatile and popular of all the sausages to cook on the smoker. You will need a few tools to make sausage: A meat grinder is essential, as is a sausage stuffer. Both of these can be found at your local sporting goods store or culinary supply store for relatively low prices. You don't need to have the most expensive model to be effective at making your own sausage. The great thing is, you can use trimmings from ribs and pork butts to make your sausage. Any pork will do, but the fattier meat will give you a better-tasting product in the end. You can take this brat recipe and add fresh jalapeños or cheese for a different twist. Adding more garlic and keeping the cloves larger is quite good as well. Have fun and make your favorite recipes.

2 eggs

1 Tbsp. chopped fresh sage

1 Tbsp. minced fresh garlic

1 Tbsp. black pepper

1 tsp. caraway seed

½ tsp. mustard powder

1 tsp. onion powder

1 tsp. paprika

5 lbs. fresh pork meat, cut into 1-inch cubes (fatty is better)

water to loosen

Mix the eggs and all the seasonings together. Mix the seasonings into the pork cubes thoroughly. Run the pork through a meat grinder on coarse grind. Mix the water in until the pork is loose and easily mixed. Presoak some sheep or hog casings. Using a sausage press, fill the casings full and fairly tight with the meat. After the casing is full, tie off the end. Divide the casing into your desired brat length. Twist the casing to separate the links. If you want to cook the links separately, let the sausage sit in the fridge for several hours and then cut the sausages at the wrap between links. To cook, place the brats on the smoker at a temperature of 275 degrees for 1 hour, turning them over once. Let them relax for at least 5 minutes before eating.

BEEF

Beef for barbecue was made famous by the cowboys in southwest Texas. Cowboys would kill a longhorn steer occasionally and slow roast the meat over a mesquite coal fire. Mexicans also barbecued beef using a pit filled with mesquite coals. For Mexicans, the head of the steer was preferred—it became known as barbacoa (Spanish for barbecue). The cowboys preferred the front shoulders, ribs, and briskets. To this day, Texas barbecue is known for barbecued beef, everything from prime rib to briskets. Beef has challenges since it has less internal fat than does pork, so it is easier to dry out. Most people start out with a brisket with moderate success. With a little knowledge and some practice, you can cook a brisket like a true Texas pitmaster.

BRISKET

Brisket is the most common beef item to be barbecued. Just the mention of brisket starts people drooling as they think of a moist, juicy brisket so tender it melts in your mouth, leaving a soft, smoky kiss behind. The packer brisket contains two major muscle groups: the flat and the point, with a layer of fat between the two muscles. The two muscles couldn't be more different. The two muscles have grains that run in opposite directions. The point is extremely fatty while the flat is very lean. The flat cooks a lot faster than the point and will often be overcooked by the time the point is done, or the point will still be tough when the flat is done. These differences cause a major problem for most people when cooking brisket. You can order the brisket separated, but the difference in price is more than double. You can separate it yourself, but this takes a lot of practice and skill to do this effectively.

Some easy-to-learn tricks will make cooking brisket a breeze. To begin, remove the full packer brisket from the cryo wrapping. Rinse off the blood left behind and pat it dry with a paper towel. Locate the large pockets of fat on the side of the brisket and underneath. Cut into the fat and remove the large chunks of fat without cutting into the meat. Using a rub with very little sugar (because briskets take a long time to cook and sugar will burn), rub the meat evenly and heavily. (When you first try making brisket, you may just want to use salt and pepper and maybe a little garlic powder.) Let the brisket relax for about 1 hour to allow the spices to set.

Heat your pit to 250 degrees and place the brisket fat side down in a direct-heat smoker or fat side up in an offset smoker. Do not touch the brisket for at least 3 hours. After 3 hours, you may want to rotate the brisket so the opposite end can be closer to the heat. Cook for another 3 hours. Lay several layers of aluminum foil on a table. Lay the brisket in the center of the top piece of foil on the opposite side it sat in the pit. (If the brisket was fat side down in the pit, you want it fat side up in the foil.) Form a boat around the brisket. Add 1 cup beef broth and 1 cup Worcestershire sauce. Wrap the brisket carefully and make sure that nothing is leaking out. (You may want to use a disposable foil pan but still wrap the brisket in foil before placing it in the foil pan, which will allow the fat to naturally separate outside of the foil with the juice left in the foil pouch you created.)

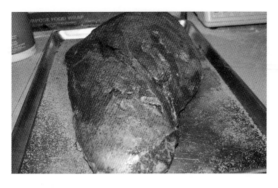 

Wrapping the brisket in foil is called the "Texas crutch." I like using this method because it cooks the brisket faster, and in my opinion the result tastes better and is more moist. However, a lot of purists will tell you that this is no way to cook a brisket. You can cook a brisket over straight smoke without ever wrapping it. The result is more rendered exterior fat and an almost-black outside crust, which a lot of people enjoy. The smoke flavor will be a lot deeper using this method as well. The two downsides to not wrapping: the brisket will take several more hours of cook time to finish, and the smoke flavor can become a bit intense (to almost over-whelming) because the meat stops absorbing smoke after 150 degrees. Feel free to try this method and decide for yourself. Whichever method you choose, you will still need to let the meat relax before you slice it.

If you decide to wrap the brisket, return the brisket to the smoker and cook for at least another 3 hours or until the temperature probe can be inserted through the brisket like Jell-O. The internal temperature should be 205 degrees, but don't go by temperature as much as by feel. When the brisket is tender, remove it from the pit, open the foil, and let it vent for at least 15 minutes. Wrap the brisket back up and let it relax for 3–4 hours in a cooler lined with newspaper on the bottom (to prevent staining your cooler). A hot holding box would work even better than a cooler. This 3–4 hours will allow the meat to relax and the juices to redistribute throughout the meat. At this point, remove the point from the flat by slicing through the fat layer between the muscles. Slice the flat into ¼-inch slices. Cut the point into cubes.

If you would like to make burnt ends, take the cubes made from the point and coat them in brown sugar and barbecue sauce. Return the cubes to the pit and cook them for at least 1 hour, stirring occasionally. The sauce and sugar will set into a crispy candy layer that has a marsh-mallow-like tenderness inside but with a blast of juicy beef. Try out the burnt ends—they will soon become a favorite!

BEEF CLODS
AND CHUCK ROLLS

Clods and chuck rolls come from the front shoulder of the beef, which, like the pork shoulder, consists of nine different muscles. These muscles have a lot of fat and collagen. They barbecue up very nicely, and, unlike the brisket, they have a very high yield of meat. They work well for cooking for large groups because the high yield gives you a lot of bang for your buck. The shoulder clod is much bigger than a brisket, with most weighing over twenty pounds. The clod takes a lot more cooking time to finish, or you can split the clod in half down the middle to create two pieces the size of briskets, with similar cooking times.

To cook the half clod, rub it down with a little oil or mustard so the spices will stick to the meat. Coat it entirely with a low-sugar rub. Let the clod relax for about 1 hour, to allow the spices to set. Heat up your pit to 250 degrees and place the clod in the smoker. Do not touch the meat for at least 3 hours. After 3 hours, you may want to rotate the clod so the opposite end can be closer to the heat. Cook for another 3 hours. Lay several layers of aluminum foil on a table. Lay the clod in the center of the top piece on the opposite side in which it sat in the pit. Form a boat around the brisket. Add 1 cup beef broth and 1 cup Worcestershire sauce. Wrap the clod carefully and make sure that nothing is leaking out. (You may want to use a disposable foil pan but still wrap the clod in foil before placing it in the foil pan, which will allow the fat to naturally separate outside of the foil with the juice left in the foil pouch you created.)

Return the clod to the smoker and cook for at least another 3 hours, up to 6, or until the temperature probe can be inserted through the brisket with little resistance. The internal temperature should be 205 degrees, but don't go by temperature as much as by feel. Let the clod relax for at least 3 hours before cutting and serving. Cut the clod into cubes and toss in your favorite barbecue sauce. Return the meat to the pit if desired; otherwise, enjoy the cubes of tender, beefy goodness.

BEEF RIBS

Whenever I see beef ribs on a smoker, I am reminded of the opening of the "Flinstones" when they place the rack of dinosaur ribs on the car tray and the car tips over. Beef ribs are enormous in comparison to pork ribs. Beef ribs are only cut from the loin back section of the rib (the same cut as the pork baby back ribs); the remainder of the ribs are too large to be effectively cooked well, so they are crosscut to make beef short ribs, which are used often in Asian cuisine. Beef ribs are not as popular as pork ribs for barbecue—the beef ribs have less fat and the rib meat is a lot more tough and difficult to get tender without overcooking. The best way to accomplish tenderness is to cook the beef ribs at a higher temperature than you would pork.

To cook beef ribs, rub them down with some type of oil and cover them liberally with your favorite rub. You can use a higher-sugar rub since it won't cook for too long. Heat the pit up to 300 degrees. Place the ribs bone side down in the pit and cook for 1–1½ hours without touching them. Tear off several sheets of foil and lay them flat on a table. Place the ribs bone side up on the foil in the center. Fold the foil up into a pouch around the ribs. Add ½ cup beef broth, ½ cup Worcestershire sauce, and ¼ cup of your favorite barbecue sauce. Close the foil up tightly, return the ribs to the pit, and allow them to cook for 1–2 hours. You should be able to insert a temperature probe through the meat with little resistance (the internal temperature will generally be between 195 and 200 degrees). When the ribs are tender, remove them from the foil and return them to the pit bone side down. Brush the ribs with barbecue sauce and cook them for 10–15 minutes until the sauce sets. Let the ribs relax for about 10 minutes before slicing and eating.

TRI-TIP ROAST

Tri-tip roasts are one of my favorite beef roasts to barbecue. Spanish cowboys in the Santa Maria region of California made barbecued tri-tips famous. Traditionally they were cooked over an open oak wood fire on a Santa Maria–style grill. Tri-tips are part of the sirloin roasts, and they are so-called because they come from the end where the three muscles in the sirloin group come together. They are also somewhat triangular in shape. The tri-tip is fairly fatty and has great flavor when barbecued. The difference between cooking a tri-tip and cooking a brisket or clod is that the tri-tip lacks collagen and should not be cooked past medium (150 degrees). If you cook it further, it will become tender but will be extremely dry and hard to eat. (The presence of collagen is what allows other meats to be cooked to 200 degrees and remain moist.)

Tri-tip will soon become one of your favorite cuts of beef to barbecue. The downside of tri-tip is it is fairly pricey to buy. If you keep your eyes open for sales and check in your grocery store for manager specials (meat that is reduced for quick sale due to time on the shelf), you can pick them up for a decent price. When you get home, if you don't want to cook them right away, wrap them heavily in a plastic wrap, making sure there is no air in the package. Then wrap them in a butcher paper before storing them in the freezer until you are ready to cook.

The day before cooking the tri-tip, make the basic brine recipe from page 76 and brine the tri-tip. Add several cloves of fresh garlic and several limes cut in half and squeezed then dropped in the brine. Also add a couple teaspoons of New Mexico chili powder. The next day remove the tri-tip from the brine and allow it to drip for a few minutes. Sprinkle a rub lightly on the outside. Heat your pit to 250 degrees and cook for 30 minutes. Turn the roast and continue cooking for another 30 minutes. Check the internal temperature of the roast. When 135 degrees is reached in the thickest part of the roast, remove it from the pit and allow it to relax for at least 15 minutes before serving. To serve the tri-tip, crosscut thin slices in the roast.

53

PRIME RIB ROASTS

I find it funny that the majority of what is labeled prime rib is not prime grade in any way, shape, or form. We have become so used to calling any slow-cooked medium-rare rib roast a prime rib that we don't bother to notice that it might be a choice-grade or even a select-grade roast. True prime ribs are very expensive and not always cost-effective to cook. I reserve buying prime-grade ribs for special occasions only. You can buy a choice-grade rib roast for a relatively decent price, but it still might be a once- or twice-a-year occasion when you can afford to do so. The great thing about the prime rib is that it has a lot of internal fat in the meat, called marbling. As the roast is slowly cooked, this fat renders and releases a ton of flavor into the meat.

For the best results in smoking a prime rib, cook it low and slow and bring it up to the desired doneness. (It is a crime against nature to cook it above an internal temperature of 145 degrees, or medium.) For the prime rib, I like to find a rib roast with the rib bones sold with it (they usually are not attached but are often sold with them). Rub the outside of the prime rib with kosher salt, fresh cracked black pepper, and cracked whole mustard seed. Let the rib roast sit for several hours to allow the salt and pepper to meld into the meat. Heat up the pit to 250 degrees and place the rib roast bone side down. Cook the rib roast for 3–5 hours, until the internal temperature is 135 degrees. (For the classic prime rib roast, cook it on a cooling rack over a foil pan to collect the juices.) Let the roast stand and relax for at least 30 minutes before serving. Serve the rib roast sliced thin, drizzled with the juices and some fresh horseradish.

CHICKEN

Barbecued chicken is very popular because it barbecues well and because many cooks like that it costs less than beef or pork. Every part of the chicken can be barbecued, but some parts work better than others. The challenge with chicken is the relatively low fat content. For this reason, legs and thighs are the most popular cut of the bird to barbecue.

WHOLE CHICKEN, HALVES, AND SPATCHCOCKED

The challenge in cooking a whole chicken is the two types of meat in the bird: the white meat of the breast and the dark meat of the thighs and legs. The white meat will cook quicker than the dark meat and will generally dry out before the dark meat is done. One way to combat this is to brine the chicken for up to 3 days before you cook. Use the basic brine recipe on page 76 and add whatever ingredients you would like for flavor; I like to add some savory spices like sage or rosemary and lemons. After you have fully brined the chicken, let it stand on a rack and drip dry for 30 minutes. Add a rub of spice under the skin and carefully remove any pockets of fat you see without breaking the skin.

Heat your smoker to 275 degrees and place the chicken breast side up. Cook for 1–3 hours, depending on the size. The internal temperature of the thigh near the bone should read 165 degrees. Let the chicken stand for 20 minutes before serving. To serve, cut the meat from the bone and pull or slice to serve.

Another way to combat the dryness in cooking whole chicken is to cut it into halves. Start by placing the bird breast side down on a cutting board. Locate the spine and start cutting from the neck region down on the side of the spine. (You can use kitchen shears if your knife skills are not where they should be to be safe.) Open the chicken carcass and locate the center of the breast bone. With a boning knife or sharp chef's knife, cut alongside the breast bone center until you have cut through the thin bone plate. When the bone plate is cut through, slice carefully through the breast and separate the two halves. Like the whole chicken, brine the halves before you cook them.

When you have seasoned the halves well, heat your smoker to 275 degrees. Place the chicken halves bone side down on the rack. Cook for 30 minutes and check the internal temperature. The breast and thigh should read 165 degrees before you pull them off. Let the halves relax for 20 minutes before cutting and serving. The advantage of cooking halves over a whole chicken is that the halves will cook a lot quicker and the white and dark meat will cook at similar times so the white meat does not dry out.

Spatchcocking the chicken offers the same ease of cooking chicken halves, but it cooks the whole bird in one piece. To spatchcock a chicken, turn the chicken breast side down on a cutting board. Locate the spine and cut to the side of the spine from the neck portion down until it is completely separated. Open up the carcass and press it firmly open until the breastbone breaks. Turn the chicken over and press the bird down toward the board until the chicken lies flat. Brine the chicken as before and cook it the same way as the chicken halves, described above.

CHICKEN THIGHS, LEGS, AND QUARTERS

Chicken thighs, legs, and quarters are the most common parts of the chicken to barbecue. They have a much higher fat content than breast meat, so they are more forgiving when you cook them and they stay moist.

Whether you are cooking leg quarters, thighs, or legs (drumsticks), the process is the same. Brine them for several hours ahead of time (or overnight) using the basic brine recipe or the poultry brine, both found on page 76. The challenge you will have cooking these cuts of meat is the skin, which has a tendency to dry out and become tough in the time it takes to cook the chicken. You can simply remove the skin if you don't want this to be an issue while cooking. Or some people will cook these cuts of meat skin side down in a disposable half pan. The natural juices from the chicken will collect in the bottom and effectively braise the skin, causing it to be tender and easy to bite through. You can cook legs and thighs straight out of the package using a rub, but I don't think the flavor will be nearly as deep or the chicken will be as moist and tender as it would be if you brine it.

To cook the chicken legs, let them drip dry for a few minutes. Peel back the skin carefully and rub them with your favorite rub or use the sweet rub on page 71. Put the skin back in place. Heat the smoker to 275 degrees. Place the legs bone side down and cook for 30 minutes. After 30 minutes, rotate them and check the internal temperature. Cook for another 30–50 minutes. The chicken should be 165 degrees against the bone. Glaze the chicken with your favorite barbecue sauce and let it cook for 10 minutes until the sauce firms up on the chicken. Let the chicken stand for several minutes before eating.

CHICKEN BREAST

Chicken breast is the most difficult cut to cook because it will dry out if you are not careful. There are two main tips that will help keep it from drying it out: first, buy breasts with the bone and skin on, and second, brine, brine, brine. If you can do both of these, it will turn out moist every time. I like to use the basic brine or the lemon-lime brine, both of which are on page 76. After the breast has been brined for at least 3 hours, let it drip for a few minutes. If you would like to add a rub, use a sweet rub like the one on page 71. But be sure to put the rub under the skin and not on top of it. Heat the pit to 300 degrees and cook for 30 minutes. Check the temperature every 10 minutes after that until the internal temperature reaches 155 degrees (the breast temperature will rise 10 degrees more when resting). Glaze the breasts with your favorite barbecue sauce and let them cook for 10 minutes until the sauce firms up on the chicken. Let the breasts relax for 10 minutes before cutting and serving.

CHICKEN WINGS

Chicken wings are amazing when they have some smoke added to them. Many places serve wings, and a lot of them would love to have a pit to use as part of the process. Wings are not too difficult to smoke; they keep nice and moist and absorb smoke well. This recipe is simple and will produce great wings every time.

2–3 lbs. chicken wings (bones in, skin on)

basic brine (page 76)

⅓ cup Frank's RedHot sauce, divided

1 cup honey

2 Tbsp. orange juice concentrate

1 Tbsp. brown mustard

blue cheese dressing, for dipping (ranch may be substituted)

The night before cooking, brine the wings in the basic brine. Add 2 tablespoons of the Frank's RedHot to the brine. Let the wings drip dry and lay them out flat in a disposable aluminum hotel pan. Heat the smoker to 300 degrees. Place the pans in the smoker and cook them for 20 minutes. Turn the wings over and cook for 20 more minutes. The internal temperature of the wings should be 165 degrees. Add the remaining ingredients, except the dressing, and stir them in well. Cook for another 10 minutes until the sauce has set on the wings. Dip into the blue cheese dressing and eat.

TURKEY, MUTTON,
AND WILD GAME

WHOLE TURKEY

During the Thanksgiving and Christmas season, I get lots of requests from people to smoke turkeys. If you have not had a smoked turkey, you may be surprised by the difference from oven-cooked turkey. The meat of smoked turkey is incredibly moist and tender, and the smoke flavor is just enough to add excitement to your everyday turkey. Turkeys are quite easy to smoke. In fact, they are no more difficult than cooking turkey in an oven. Follow the directions in the whole chicken section (page 56) if you would like to halve or spatchcock your turkey. This will allow it to cook better, with the dark meat and light meat cooking for about the same time so they are equally moist. Whether you are smoking it or not, brining the turkey is of utmost importance. This will give you much more flavor and allow the meat to be a lot more moist. The following recipe has taken me a long time to develop.

2 liters ginger ale

2 liters water

1 cup kosher salt

1 cup brown sugar

¼ cup black pepper

1 cup zesty Italian dressing

¼ cup cider vinegar

2 Tbsp. maple extract flavoring

1 (12- to 20-lb.) whole turkey

Mix the ginger ale, water, kosher salt, brown sugar, black pepper, Italian dressing, cider vinegar, and maple extract together. Brine the turkey for 1–3 days. For brining, I like to use a 5-gallon water cooler lined with a trash bag with ice underneath. This will keep it cool, as long as I change out the ice every day, and I don't have to take up fridge space. Remove the turkey from the brine and let it drip dry for a few minutes. Heat your pit to 275 degrees. Cook the turkey for 2–3 hours. Check the internal temperature—the probe should read about 135 degrees when inserted near the bone. Place the turkey in a disposable aluminum hotel pan and wrap with foil or high-temperature plastic wrap. Cook the turkey for 1 more hour and check the internal temperature again. The temperature of the thigh should be close to 180 degrees, and the breasts should be 165 degrees. Let the turkey stand for 20 minutes before carving and serving.

TURKEY LEGS

Many people come back from Disneyland talking about the smoked turkey legs and how good they were. There are a lot of truck stops that also sell a version of them, though not as tasty. Smoked turkey legs are quite simple to make. The good thing about cooking the legs is that they have a lot of fat and moisture in the meat, so they are forgiving to cook.

2 liters lemon-lime soda

1 cup orange juice

1 cup soy sauce

½ cup brown sugar

5–7 lbs. turkey legs

Combine the lemon-lime soda, orange juice, soy sauce, and brown sugar. Let the turkey legs sit in the brine in the refrigerator for a minimum of 3–5 days. Heat up your smoker to 250 degrees. Cook the legs for 3 hours, turning them every hour. Check the internal temperature. It will be done at 180 degrees. If it hasn't reached 180 yet, continue cooking until it does. Let the legs relax for up to 30 minutes before eating. They are also great if you chill them completely and then reheat them before eating. This redistributes and intensifies the flavor.

MUTTON

Mutton is popular in areas around Kentucky, where it is the traditional meat used for barbecue. The popularity of barbecued mutton has not spread far beyond that region, with the exception of New Zealand and Australia, where it is an extremely popular meat to cook. I myself have not smoked a lot of mutton, but I have cooked enough to know how to do it. The advantage mutton has over a lot of different meats is a lot of fat and collagen, which makes for some great barbecue. The disadvantage is that mutton tastes like mutton—some people don't enjoy the flavor. However, brining mutton with the following recipe will give it great flavor that you will enjoy. Mutton may become one of your favorites to barbecue.

½ gallon water

1½ cup Worcestershire sauce, divided

¼ cup kosher salt

¼ cup brown sugar

¼ cup black pepper

1 cup chopped shiitake mushrooms

1 leg of lamb

½ cup beef broth

Combine the water, 1 cup Worcestershire sauce, kosher salt, brown sugar, black pepper, and mushrooms. Let the leg of lamb sit in the brine for 1–3 days. Heat the pit to 250 degrees. Cook the leg for 3–5 hours, turning it over every hour until the meat reaches 160 degrees. Lay some foil on a table. Lay the leg of lamb in the foil and fold the foil into a boat to hold liquid. Pour in ½ cup Worcestershire sauce and the beef broth. Return the leg of lamb to the pit and cook for 1–3 hours until the meat reaches 200 degrees. Remove the meat from the pit, open the foil, and allow it to vent for 15 minutes. Let the meat stand in a cooler lined with newspaper or a hot box for at least an hour and up to 4 hours before you serve it. You can slice, pull, or cube the meat. Add barbecue sauce to the juice left in the foil and drizzle it on the meat or toss the leg meat into it.

WILD GAME

Through the majority of the year, my family eats mostly game meat. Whether it be elk, deer, moose, or wild pig, it is the meat that we prefer to eat. It is healthy, and, with the exception of the wild pig, it is low fat. Even wild pig is much lower in fat than domestic hog. Because the meat is so much lower in fat, it is a lot more difficult to barbecue. If you are cooking wild pig, use the same directions as above in the hog section of this chapter, except you need to reduce your cook times a little because it will cook a lot quicker than regular hog. If you are cooking deer, elk, moose, or any other red wild game meat, the complete lack of fat will not allow you to cook it to a high temperature without drying it out. You should use roasts when you smoke the game since it will help you keep the meat moist.

Brine the game meat using the basic brine recipe on page 76. Heat the pit to 225 degrees. Check the internal temperature of the meat every 30 minutes. You should pull the game meat out at an internal temperature of 145 degrees. Let the meat relax for 15 minutes before cutting and slicing. This meat will not pull, so the best method is to slice it thin to serve.

BARBECUE RUBS, SAUCES, AND MARINADES

RUBS AND SAUCES

RUBS

Barbecue rubs are as diverse as they are plentiful. Literally thousands of rubs are commercially available, and it would be impossible for me to tell you which one will work the best for your tastes. My favorite go-to rub is Tony Chachere's creole seasoning. It is good on almost all types of meats, and it works well for side dishes as well. In fact, there is not much that I don't use Tony's on when I cook. Some commercial rubs are specialized for beef, pork, chicken, and game, in addition to all-around rubs. One of the biggest thrills in barbecue is to create your own rubs and discover which one will work the best for you. A great rub will contain a balance of the following elements: sweet, salty, spicy, and tangy. If you can create a rub that contains all four and tastes good with the meat, you will have a winning recipe. Many barbecue competitors have created great rubs with which they have competed and won. They then market and sell the rub, which is part of the reason there are so many rubs available.

The following is a list of spices that are commonly used in barbecue rubs:

Salt*	Paprika	New Mexico chili powder
Sugar	Smoked paprika	Celery seed
Brown sugar	Chili powder	Oregano
Honey powder	Onion powder	Sage
Maple sugar	Garlic powder	Mustard seed
Natural sugar (Turbinado)	Black pepper	Nutmeg
Tomato powder	White pepper	
Cinnamon	Chipotle powder	

*Sea salt and kosher salt are most popular

You will need to keep several things in mind. A rub that tastes good on your hand will not always taste good when it is cooked. It is wise to have a piece of meat and a hot skillet standing by to test out your rub before you finalize it. You also need to determine if you want to use the rub for a slow cook versus a quick cook since too much sugar will cause the rub to burn.

BASIC BARBECUE RUB

This rub is a good all-around rub for cooking almost everything barbecue, and it is a good starting point.

¼ cup sea salt

3 Tbsp. white sugar

1 Tbsp. brown sugar

2 tsp. onion powder

2 tsp. garlic powder

1 Tbsp. paprika

2 tsp. black pepper

Put all the ingredients into a container with a lid. Close the lid and shake and tumble until the ingredients are mixed thoroughly. To use the rub, apply generously to your meat. After the meat sits for about 10 minutes, shake off any remaining rub before cooking.

PORK RIB RUB

¼ cup brown sugar

3 Tbsp. sea salt

2 Tbsp. paprika

1 Tbsp. black pepper

1 tsp. white pepper

Put all the ingredients into a container with a lid. Close the lid and shake and tumble until the ingredients are mixed thoroughly. To use the rub, apply generously to your meat. After the meat sits for about 10 minutes, shake off any remaining rub before cooking.

BEEF AND GAME RUB

¼ cup sea salt

1 Tbsp. brown sugar

1 Tbsp. onion powder

1 Tbsp. garlic powder

1 Tbsp. black pepper

2 Tbsp. smoked paprika

1 tsp. celery seed

Put all the ingredients into a container with a lid. Close the lid and shake and tumble until the ingredients are mixed thoroughly. To use the rub, apply generously to your meat. After the meat sits for about 10 minutes, shake off any remaining rub before cooking.

CHICKEN RUB

¼ cup honey sugar

2 Tbsp. sea salt

1 Tbsp. paprika

1 tsp. garlic

1 tsp. oregano

½ tsp. sage

Put all the ingredients into a container with a lid. Close the lid and shake and tumble until the ingredients are mixed thoroughly. To use the rub, apply generously to your meat. After the meat sits for about 10 minutes, shake off any remaining rub before cooking.

PORK RUB

¼ cup salt

¼ cup paprika

3 Tbsp. brown sugar

2 tsp. garlic

1 tsp. onion powder

1 tsp. sage

2 tsp. black pepper

Put all the ingredients into a container with a lid. Close the lid and shake and tumble until the ingredients are mixed thoroughly. To use the rub, apply generously to your meat. After the meat sits for about 10 minutes, shake off any remaining rub before cooking.

SWEET RUB

¼ cup sea salt

⅓ cup turbinado (natural) sugar

2 Tbsp. black pepper

¼ tsp. ground red pepper

2 tsp. smoked sweet paprika

1 tsp. granulated garlic

½ tsp. granulated onion

Put all the ingredients into a container with a lid. Close the lid and shake and tumble until the ingredients are mixed thoroughly. This rub has a log of sugar and should be used as a finish rub. Otherwise, the sugar can burn while cooking and give your meat a black skin.

SAUCES

Barbecue sauces are as unique as they are diverse. There is really no right or wrong way to make a barbecue sauce. Barbecue sauces vary greatly depending on what part of the country you are in. In the Carolinas, barbecue sauces are vinegar based and thin. In Kansas City, barbecue sauces are sugar based with tomato and are thick. Most commercial barbecue sauces lean toward the Kansas City style. In Texas, bold and spicy barbecue sauces are the norm.

When you make a barbecue sauce, you can start with many different bases and experiment from there. Ketchup is one of the most common starting points in creating a barbecue sauce. Tomato juice, tomato paste, jams, and jellies are all popular starting points for barbecue sauce as well. I personally prefer not to use ketchup because I think it is difficult to keep the ketchup taste out of your barbecue sauce. Sweetness in barbecue sauces can be achieved by using corn syrup, honey, molasses, brown sugar, sugars dissolved in water, and agave nectars. Often, natural fruits may be used to sweeten and enhance sauces. The following recipes are simply starting points to get you on the right track. Many barbecue competitors will use popular commercial sauces as their base, which they doctor to suit their tastes and style.

BASIC BARBECUE SAUCE

1 cup ketchup

1 cup honey

3 Tbsp. molasses

2 Tbsp. Worcestershire sauce

2 tsp. black pepper

1 tsp. white pepper

2 tsp. liquid smoke

¼ cup apple cider vinegar

Mix all the ingredients in a blender and then heat in a saucepan to a soft boil. Cool down.

BOLD AND SPICY SAUCE

½ cup raisins

½ cup apple cider vinegar

½ cup tomato paste

2 Tbsp. molasses

1 cup dark Karo syrup

3 tsp. black pepper

1 tsp. ground red pepper

2 tsp. onion powder

1 tsp. garlic powder

2 Tbsp. Worcestershire sauce

2 Tbsp. brown mustard

1 tsp. salt

In a saucepan, boil the raisins and apple cider vinegar for 10 minutes. Pour mixture into a food processor or blender and blend thoroughly. Add the remaining ingredients and puree for several minutes. Return mixture to the saucepan and heat to a boil before letting it cool down for use.

73

SWEET SAUCE

1 cup seedless jam (raspberry or blackberry)

¼ cup tomato paste

½ cup brown sugar

3 Tbsp. molasses

¼ cup orange juice concentrate

1 tsp. black pepper

¼ cup corn syrup or honey

1 tsp. salt

Puree everything in a blender. Heat mixture in a saucepan and then let it cool down for use.

CAROLINA-STYLE SAUCE

1 cup cider vinegar

½ cup water

½ cup brown sugar

2 tsp. salt

1 cup tomato juice

2 tsp. onion powder

Mix ingredients in a saucepan and heat on the stove.

BRINES AND MARINADES

As mentioned in previous chapters, I like to use brines in a lot of what I do. The way a brine works is it preserves the outside membrane of the cell structure, so when the meat cooks, the liquid inside is trapped and will not dry out the meat. A brine also adds flavoring throughout the meat. In some instances where acids are used in a brine, it will help tenderize the meat.

A marinade is different from a brine in that you are generally just adding flavor to the meat. Marinades work especially well in a meat with a high fat content. They work by absorbing flavors into the fat that are released into the meat when the fat renders while cooking.

TANDOORI CHICKEN MARINADE

3 cups plain greek yogurt

1 onion, sliced

3 Tbsp. curry powder

2 tsp. salt

1 cup water

1 tsp. black pepper

HONEY APRICOT MARINADE

2 cup water

1 cup apricot jam

2 tsp. salt

¼ cup honey

2 tsp. black pepper

BASIC BRINE

1 gallon cold water

1 cup kosher salt

1 cup sugar

POULTRY BRINE

2 liters ginger ale

2 liters water

1 cup kosher salt

1 cup zesty Italian dressing

½ cup cider vinegar

1 cup brown sugar

¼ cup black pepper

2 Tbsp. maple flavoring extract

LEMON-LIME BRINE

2 liters lemon-lime soda

2 cups soy sauce

3 Tbsp. black pepper

COLA BRINE

2 liters Coca-Cola or other cola

½ cup soy sauce

½ cup Worcestershire sauce

¼ cup black pepper

2 Tbsp. onion powder

9

BARBECUE SIDE DISHES AND DESSERTS

SIDES AND DESSERTS

Icouldn't do a barbecue book and not include a few side dish and dessert recipes that go along so well with barbecue. A lot of these are classic dishes from the South. I hope you enjoy them.

SOUTHERN-STYLE CORN BREAD

2 Tbsp. bacon grease or vegetable oil

1 cup white cornmeal

2 cups buttermilk

1¾ cups white flour

1½ tsp. baking powder

1 tsp. baking soda

½ tsp. cream of tartar

1 tsp. salt

⅓ cup white sugar

⅓ cup brown sugar

3 large eggs

2 Tbsp. honey

4 Tbsp. butter, melted

2 cups fresh or frozen corn kernels (do not use canned corn)

½ lb. cooked bacon, chopped (optional)

Preheat oven to 375 degrees. Grease a half-size hotel pan with the bacon grease. In a bowl, mix all the remaining ingredients together and pour into the hotel pan. (For an extra-fluffy corn bread, soak the cornmeal in the buttermilk the night before and then mix everything else together.) Bake for 40–50 minutes, or until you can insert a knife in the center and have it come out clean.

SOUTHWESTERN-STYLE CORN BREAD

6–10 jalapeño peppers, depending on the size (should be ¾ cup once roasted and diced)

1½ cups yellow cornmeal

2½ cups milk

1½ cups white flour

1½ tsp. baking powder

1½ tsp. baking soda

½ tsp. cream of tartar

2 tsp. salt

½ cup white sugar

½ cup brown sugar

3 large eggs

8 Tbsp. butter, melted

1 cup frozen corn kernels

Slice the jalapeños in half and remove the veins and seeds. Roast the jalapeños in a skillet for 15–20 minutes, or until they are starting to brown. Remove from the pan and dice them into small pieces. Preheat oven to 350 degrees. Grease a disposable, aluminum, half-size hotel pan. In a bowl, mix all the ingredients together and pour into the hotel pan. Bake for 40–50 minutes, or until you can insert a knife in the center and have it come out clean.

SOUTHERN CREAMED CORN IN A DUTCH OVEN

This is nothing like the slimy, canned stuff. It goes well with almost any meat dish.

2 Tbsp. butter

2 Tbsp. flour

2/3 cup milk

1 (16-oz.) pkg. frozen
sweet corn

2 tsp. sugar

1/2 pint cream

1 tsp. salt

Place the coals in a checkerboard pattern underneath the Dutch oven. Use the same amount of coals as the size of your Dutch oven—e.g., if you are using a 12-inch Dutch oven, use 12 coals. Melt the butter in the bottom of a Dutch oven. Whisk the flour in a little at a time until it is covered well. Slowly pour in the milk and bring it to a boil. Add the corn, sugar, cream, and salt. Stir in and simmer for 15 minutes. The corn should be tender.

CLASSIC COLESLAW

Coleslaw, like barbecue, has a million different ways to make it, with many families having their own way of doing things. This recipe is one of the best I have tried.

1 cup real mayonnaise

1 cup sour cream

1/2 cup white sugar

1/4 cup white vinegar

3 Tbsp. Frank's RedHot
sauce

1 Tbsp. creamy
horseradish

2 heads of cabbage,
finely shredded

Mix all the ingredients together except the cabbage. Fold the mixture into the cabbage. Let the coleslaw chill for at least 1 hour before serving to allow all the spices to meld.

NORTHERN SWEET CORN BREAD

1½ cups yellow
 cornmeal

1½ cups milk

1½ cups white flour

1½ tsp. baking powder

1½ tsp. baking soda

½ tsp. cream of tartar

1½ tsp. salt

1 cup brown sugar

3 large eggs

1 stick butter, melted

1 cup boiling water

Preheat oven to 375 degrees. Grease a disposable, aluminum, half-size hotel pan. In a bowl, mix all the ingredients together except the water. Slowly add the water and mix well. Pour mixture into the hotel pan. Bake for 40–50 minutes, or until you can insert a knife in the center and have it come out clean.

SOUTHERN-STYLE POTATO CASSEROLE

This is my number one requested recipe from the many catering jobs that I do. It is slightly spicy but not so bad that it can't be enjoyed by most people. If you are sensitive to spicy foods, you can cut the creole seasoning in half and add two teaspoons of salt instead.

3 lbs. potatoes, diced small

1 cup sour cream

1 cup milk

2 Tbsp. Tony Chachere's creole seasoning to taste

½ lb. ham, cubed small

½ lb. shredded cheddar cheese

Preheat oven to 375 degrees. Mix the potatoes and the creole seasoning together. Add the sour cream and milk. Stir it well. Fold the ham and the cheese into the potatoes. Place in a disposable, aluminum, half-size hotel pan. Bake for about 1 hour. The cheese should all be melted and starting to brown.

HUSH PUPPIES

Hush puppies are a southern favorite and go great with a barbecue. Make sure that you use a sweet onion and these will become a favorite.

- 1–1½ cups cornmeal
- ½ cup flour
- ¼ cup sugar
- 1 tsp. salt
- 1 tsp. baking soda
- 1 cup buttermilk
- 1 egg
- ½ sweet onion cut into small slices

Mix all the ingredients together except the onion. The batter should be stiff enough to form a ball with. If it is not stiff enough, add flour a little at a time. Fold the onions in. Heat up some vegetable oil in a pan to 350 degrees. Using a spoon, spoon out the dough into ping-pong-size balls. Carefully lower them into the oil using a slotted spoon. Fry them until they are browned. Set them on a paper towel to drain and wait 5 minutes before serving.

CREAMED CHEESY SPINACH

This is one of my family's favorite side dishes. Using fresh spinach is the best, but make sure to rinse it well.

- 2 Tbsp. real butter
- 3 lbs. baby spinach leaves, rinsed well and left whole
- ¼ cup cider vinegar
- 2 cups chicken stock
- 1 cup sour cream
- 1 cup shredded cheddar cheese
- salt and pepper to taste

Melt the butter in a skillet. Add the spinach, vinegar, and chicken stock. Cover and cook on medium heat until the liquid is almost gone. Stir in the sour cream and cook it for 2 minutes. Stir in the cheese a little at a time until the cheese is melted. Add salt and pepper to taste. Let it relax for 5 minutes before serving.

FOUR-CHEESE MAC AND CHEESE

Mac and cheese is an American classic developed in colonial times. This recipe is vastly different than the instant style we are so accustomed to. I love the rich and creamy texture and flavor. It goes well with almost every meat dish.

8 oz. elbow macaroni

4 Tbsp. butter

4 Tbsp. flour

3 cups milk

1 tsp. salt

pepper to taste

1 egg, whipped (optional)

4 oz. shredded sharp cheddar cheese

8 oz. shredded Colby Jack cheese

4 oz. Velveeta cheese

4 oz. cream cheese

Preheat oven to 375 degrees. Boil the macaroni and remove them al dente. If you cook them more, they will overcook when you bake. In the bottom of a saucepan, melt the butter and whisk in the flour until there are no lumps. Slowly whisk in the milk, salt, and pepper. Whisk in the egg (optional) and all of the shredded and processed cheese, except a small amount to sprinkle on top before baking. Stir in the cheese and fold in the noodles. Pour the noodles and cheese into a half-size, aluminum, disposable hotel pan. Bake for 20–30 minutes, depending on the doneness you desire. Let it sit for 5 minutes before serving.

FROM-SCRATCH BAKED BEANS

1–1½ lbs. bacon, cut into small pieces (I prefer to use the ends-and-pieces packages available at the grocery store)

2 lbs. dried pinto beans

¼ cup white sugar

¼ cup barbecue sauce

¼ cup brown sugar

¼ cup cider vinegar

¼ cup Frank's RedHot sauce

1 onion, peeled and left whole

water to cover the beans (and added continually as needed)

salt to taste

Add all the ingredients to a full-size, disposable, aluminum hotel pan. Cover with foil. If you are cooking in your pit, place the beans in the coolest part of the pit and cook for up to 12 hours. If you cook in the oven, bake it at 400 degrees for 3–5 hours, checking every hour for liquid level and adding liquid when needed.

ATOMIC BUFFALO TURDS

This is one of those staple recipes in the barbecue world. Despite the name, these are very good to eat for the adventurous.

2–3 lbs. fresh jalapeño peppers

1 pkg. string cheese sticks

1 lb. bacon

Slice the peppers in half and remove the veins and seeds. Cut a piece of the cheese stick to fit inside the pepper. Wrap the pepper in bacon and pin it together with a toothpick. Cook on the smoker or the grill until the bacon is done and a little crispy. Let them cool for 5 minutes before eating.

COLLARD GREENS

I love greens, and they are quite common in barbecue. The trick to the greens is to roll them in your hand for several minutes before cutting them up and cooking them. This will help break down the fibrous leaves and add a sweetness to your dish.

2–3 lbs. collared greens (or mustard greens)

½ lb. bacon, cut into small pieces

½ cup cider vinegar

3 Tbsp. Frank's RedHot sauce

¼ cup brown sugar

28 oz. chicken stock

salt to taste

Roll the leaves of greens in your hand until they are dark green. Cut the greens into strips and set aside. Brown the bacon in the bottom of a heavy saucepan or Dutch oven. Add the greens and the remaining ingredients. Cook on medium heat for 2–5 hours, adding water occasionally to keep the liquid level to the top of the greens. When you are ready to serve, let the water level subside until it is almost gone.

BLACK-EYED PEAS

Black-eyed peas are quite popular in some parts of the country. If possible, use fresh peas for the best results. If you can't find fresh, frozen peas work well, and canned is okay if they are drained and rinsed first.

¼ lb. bacon, cut into small pieces

1 small onion, sliced thin

5 cups black-eyed peas

2 garlic cloves, whole

28 oz. chicken stock

salt and pepper to taste

In a saucepan or Dutch oven, brown the bacon and the onions. Stir in the remaining ingredients. Simmer on medium-low heat, covered, for 2 hours, adding water if needed. Remove garlic cloves before serving.

SMOKED MEATLOAF

Meatloaf is amazing smoked. I like mine a little bit spicy, but if you don't like them spicy, take out the peppers.

2 lbs. ground beef

1 lb.ground sweet Italian sausage

1 small onion

4–5 fresh jalapenos, seeded, veined, and chopped

1 cup Italian-style breadcrumbs

2 cloves garlic, minced

2 large eggs

¼ cup Worcestershire sauce

1 lb. bacon to wrap (optional)

Mix all the ingredients except the sauce (and optional bacon) together. Form a loaf. If you use the bacon, wrap the pieces around the loaf. Cook in the smoker for 1 hour at 300 degrees. Wrap the meat in foil and add the Worcestershire sauce. Cook for another 30 minutes and check the internal temperature—it should be 160 degrees. Let the meat sit for 20 minutes in the foil before eating.

CLASSIC POTATO SALAD

I don't think there is anything I like better than barbecue, potato salad, and corn on the cob on a hot summer evening. This is classic and, in my opinion, the best.

3 lbs. russet potatoes

8 eggs

½ cup sweet pickle relish or pickles cut small

1 cup real mayonnaise (not light)

3 Tbsp. Frank's RedHot sauce

¼ cup yellow mustard

Tony Chachere's creole seasoning to taste

Cube the potatoes and boil them until they are tender. Strain them and run cold water over them to chill. Place them in the fridge for several hours before making the salad. Boil the eggs for 15 minutes. Run them over with cold water. Peel and finely chop the eggs. In a large bowl, mix all the ingredients together except the potatoes. Fold in the potatoes until they are covered with the rest. The more you stir them, the smaller the potato chunks will be. Chill the salad and sprinkle some paprika or barbecue rub over the salad to garnish it.

PECAN PIE

While traveling through the South, I fell in love with pecan pie. A lot of this love came from the fresh pecans growing all over. I have tried a number of recipes, yet this is the one I like the best. It is not the healthiest recipe, but it's great for a once-in-a-while treat. For a Hawaiian twist on this, substitute the pecans for macadamia nuts.

FOR THE CRUST:

3 cups flour

1 tsp. salt

1½ cups shortening
(I prefer butter flavor)

1 egg, whipped

5 Tbsp. cold water
(ice water is even
better)

1 Tbsp. white vinegar

FOR THE FILLING:

4 eggs, slightly beaten

1 cup dark corn syrup

²/₃ cup sugar

½ cup butter, melted

1 tsp. vanilla

1¼ cups chopped
pecans or pecan
halves

CRUST: Sift the flour and salt together. Using a pastry cutter, cut the shortening into the flour until the fat is pebbled about the size of a pea. In a bowl, mix the egg, water, and vinegar. Pour the water mixture over the top of the flour and salt mixture. Knead the dough together until it will hold together and no more. The dough works better if you have time to chill it at this point. Roll the dough out onto floured parchment paper for easy working. Use flour between your rolling pin and the pastry if it is starting to pull. Place the pastry in a lightly oiled pie tin (line the pie tin with a parchment round and strips if you want to remove the pie from the pan). Fill the pastry with the filling (see below) and bake until the pastry is golden. (If you want to have a shiny pastry top, use an egg wash: mix 1 egg with 2 tablespoons water. Brush the top of the pastry before cooking.)

FILLING: Preheat oven to 350 degrees. Mix the ingredients together and pour into the open-faced pie shell. Bake for 35–40 minutes. You should be able to insert a knife into the center and have it come out clean.

RED VELVET CAKE

It would seem wrong for me to write a recipe book on southern-style cooking and not include a recipe for a true southern classic. Red velvet cake is great tasting but very rich.

2 cups flour

2 cups white sugar

3 Tbsp. cocoa

1–1½ tsp. baking powder

1–1½ tsp. baking soda

1 tsp. salt

3 eggs

1 cup milk

½ cups real butter, melted

2 tsp. vanilla

1 cup boiling water

Preheat the oven to 375 degrees. Mix all the ingredients together except the water for 5 minutes. Slowly add the boiling water and mix well. Pour mixture into a well-greased cake pan. Bake for 45 minutes. Do not check the cake prior to 45 minutes. It will collapse in the center. When you tap the pan, the cake should jiggle like well-set Jell-O. If the cake seems too loose, continue cooking until it has set. Let the cake cool completely before frosting with a cream cheese frosting (see below).

CREAM CHEESE FROSTING

8 oz. cream cheese, room temperature

1 tsp. vanilla

powdered sugar (enough to reach desired consistency)

Mix ingredients together well with a blender until the frosting is smooth and the flavor you desire is reached.

APPLE CRISP

Apple crisp is a southern favorite. It is best cooked in a Dutch oven! It's hard to beat a hot crisp covered in vanilla ice cream.

FOR THE FILLING:

6 cups sliced apples

2 Tbsp. flour

1 tsp. cinnamon

½ tsp. nutmeg

½ cup brown sugar, packed

½ cup white sugar

FOR THE CRISP:

¾ cup rolled oats

¾ cup flour

½ tsp. salt

6 Tbsp. butter

Preheat oven to 375 degrees. Mix the filling ingredients together. Set them in the bottom of a 9-inch baking pan. For the crisp, mix the oats, flour, and salt in a bowl. Cut the butter in with a pastry cutter. Sprinkle the crisp over the top of the filling. Bake for 30 minutes. Let it relax for 15 minutes before serving.

FRESH PEACH COBBLER

This is not your Scoutmaster's cobbler! In Utah, we grow amazing peaches. This is so good that it's tempting to have it every day during peach season.

FOR THE PEACHES:

6–10 fresh peaches, sliced (it should measure about 5 cups)

1–1½ cups white sugar

¼ cup flour

1 pinch cinnamon

FOR THE TOPPING:

3 cups flour

¾ cup sugar

1½ tsp. baking powder

1 tsp. salt

1–1½ cups butter

½ cup milk, warmed

¼ cup buttermilk

cinnamon and sugar to taste

Combine all of the ingredients for the peaches together. If using a Dutch oven, place a ring of charcoal around the bottom underneath and a checkerboard pattern on the lid. Use a 12-inch Dutch oven and use 16 coals on the top and 12 coals underneath. Bake for 15 minutes in the Dutch oven. Or if using an oven, bake at 375 degrees in a disposable, aluminum, half-size hotel pan. In the meantime, for the topping, mix the flour, sugar, baking powder, and salt together. Cut in the butter with a pastry cutter. Slowly stir in the warm milk and the buttermilk. Drop spoonfuls of the topping on top of the peaches. (Or roll out flat and cut out like biscuits, and then put biscuits on top of peaches.) Sprinkle cinnamon and sugar on top of the cobbler. Bake for 1 hour. The cobbler should be browned. Let it relax for 10 minutes before serving.

COMPETITION BARBECUE AND ORGANIZATIONS

If you begin to barbecue and you get hooked, a number of venues are available for expanding and developing your passion. Competitive barbecue is not for everybody, but many people, once they start, are hooked for life. I have heard competitive barbecue called "high-stakes redneck gambling," and I suppose in a way it is. Winning isn't always a guarantee. In fact, if you can break even in most competitions, you are doing well. What you will find in competitive barbecue is a large family of barbecue enthusiasts who are ready to welcome you to the family.

Several organizations host competitions. The KCBS, or Kansas City Barbecue Society, is probably the largest. There are many others as well: The MBN, or Memphis

Barbecue Network; and the IBCA, International Barbecue Cookers Association. Many local organizations in your area can help you out as well. In my area I am a managing member of the Utah BBQ Organization. We host ten barbecue cook-offs every year, both backyard and pro divisions.

Barbecue enthusiasts also share information on many websites, including

- utahbbq.org
- bbq-brethren.com
- thesmokering.com

These forums will answer any questions you may have.

I hope this book has helped you out, with its minimal learning curve and barbecue secrets. I hope the barbecue bug takes over and I see you at a competition as a competitor, a judge, or a spectator!

INDEX

A

apple crisp: 96

atomic buffalo turds: 90

B

baby back ribs: 44–45

basic barbecue rub: 70

basic barbecue sauce: 72

basic brine: 76

beef and game rub: 70

beef clods and chuck rolls: 51

beef ribs: 52

black-eyed peas: 91

black pepper bacon: 30

black pepper jerky: 24

bold and spicy sauce: 73

brisket: 49–50

C

cajun-style smoked fish: 20

Canadian bacon: 30

Carolina-style sauce: 74

chicken breast: 60

chicken rub: 71

chicken thighs, legs, and quarters: 58

chicken wings: 61

classic coleslaw: 81

classic potato salad: 93

cola brine: 76

cola smoked fish: 20

collard greens: 91

country-style bacon: 28

cream cheese frosting: 95

creamed cheesy spinach: 85

D

Dad's jerky: 24

F

four-cheese mac and cheese: 87

fresh bratwurst: 46

fresh peach cobbler: 98

from-scratch baked beans: 88

H

honey apricot marinade: 76

hush puppies: 85

L

lemon-lime brine: 76

lox: 19

M

maple-cured bacon: 31

modern ham: 29

mutton: 65

N

northern sweet corn bread: 82

O

old-fashioned jerky: 23

P

pecan pie: 94

pork rib rub: 70

pork rub: 71

pork shoulder: 39–40

poultry brine: 76

prime rib roasts: 54

R

red velvet cake: 95

S

smoked cheese: 32

smoked meatloaf: 92

smoked turkey breast: 31

southern creamed corn in a
Dutch oven: 81

southern-style corn bread: 79

southern-style potato
casserole: 84

southwestern-style corn bread: 80

St. Louis–style ribs: 42–43

sweet barbecue jerky: 25

sweet rub: 71

sweet sauce: 73

T

tandoori chicken marinade: 76

teriyaki jerky: 23

teriyaki-style smoked fish: 21

traditional jerky: 23

traditional smoked salmon: 21

tri-tip roast: 53

turkey ham: 31

turkey legs: 64

V

Virginia ham: 27

W

whole chicken, halves, and
    spatchcocked: 56–57

whole hog: 35–38

whole hog injection: 38

whole turkey: 63

wild game: 66

103

Cooking Measurement Equivalents

Cups	Tablespoons	Fluid Ounces
⅛ cup	2 Tbsp.	1 fl. oz.
¼ cup	4 Tbsp.	2 fl. oz.
⅓ cup	5 Tbsp. + 1 tsp.	
½ cup	8 Tbsp.	4 fl. oz.
⅔ cup	10 Tbsp. + 2 tsp.	
¾ cup	12 Tbsp.	6 fl. oz.
1 cup	16 Tbsp.	8 fl. oz.

Cups	Fluid Ounces	Pints/Quarts/Gallons
1 cup	8 fl. oz.	½ pint
2 cups	16 fl. oz.	1 pint = ½ quart
3 cups	24 fl. oz.	1½ pints
4 cups	32 fl. oz.	2 pints = 1 quart
8 cups	64 fl. oz.	2 quarts = ½ gallon
16 cups	128 fl. oz.	4 quarts = 1 gallon

Other Helpful Equivalents

1 Tbsp.	3 tsp.
8 oz.	½ lb.
16 oz.	1 lb.

Metric Measurement Equivalents

Approximate Weight Equivalents

Ounces	Pounds	Grams
4 oz.	¼ lb.	113 g
5 oz.		142 g
6 oz.		170 g
8 oz.	½ lb.	227 g
9 oz.		255 g
12 oz.	¾ lb.	340 g
16 oz.	1 lb.	454 g

Approximate Volume Equivalents

Cups	US Fluid Ounces	Milliliters
⅛ cup	1 fl. oz.	30 ml
¼ cup	2 fl. oz.	59 ml
½ cup	4 fl. oz.	118 ml
¾ cup	6 fl. oz.	177 ml
1 cup	8 fl. oz.	237 ml

Other Helpful Equivalents

½ tsp.	2½ ml
1 tsp.	5 ml
1 Tbsp.	15 ml

MATT PELTON

AUTHOR OF FROM MOUNTAINTOP TO TABLETOP

THE CAST IRON CHEF

MAIN COURSES

FROM MOUNTAINTOP TO TABLETOP

THE COMPLETE GUIDE TO COOKING WILD GAME

MATT PELTON

ABOUT THE AUTHOR

MATT PELTON grew up in central Utah where he learned the art of Dutch oven cooking. He brought his passion with him on a two-year mission to Boston for The Church of Jesus Christ of Latter-day Saints; he packed his ten-inch Dutch oven in his suitcase. At every opportunity, he learned to cook food from the many cultures in the Boston area. When he returned home, he met and married his wife of fourteen years, Katie. They have three wonderful children: Megan, age twelve; Tristan, age ten; and Braxton, age five. Matt was bitten by the bug of competitive cooking and has competed in the Kansas City Barbecue Society pro-division barbecue competitions. He also competes in the International Dutch Oven Society's advanced cooking circuit where he and his cooking partner, Doug Martin, won the 2012 IDOS World Championship. Matt travels around the West competing and teaching Dutch oven classes. His previous books are *From Mountaintop to Tabletop*, *The Cast Iron Chef*, and *The Cast Iron Gourmet*.